DISINTEGRATING EUROPE

DISINTEGRATING EUROPE

The Twilight of the European Construction

NORIKO HAMA

Westport, Connecticut

330.94
H19d

Published in the United States and Canada by Praeger Publishers
88 Post Road West, Westport, CT 06881
An imprint of Greenwood Publishing Group, Inc.

Printed in the United States of America

The paper used in this book complies with the
Permanent Paper Standard issued by the National
Information Standards Organization (Z39.48–1984).

10 9 8 7 6 5 4 3 2 1

English language edition, except the United States and Canada,
published by Adamantine Press Limited, 3 Henrietta Street, Covent
Garden, London WC2E 8LU England.

First published in 1996

Library of Congress Cataloging-in-Publication Data

Hama, Noriko.
    Disintegrating Europe : the twilight of the European construction
/ Noriko Hama.
       p.   cm.—(Praeger studies on the 21st century, ISSN
1070–1850)
    Includes bibliographical references and index.
    ISBN 0–275–95582–6 (alk. paper).—ISBN 0–275–95581–8 (pbk. :
alk. paper)
    1. Economic forecasting—Europe. 2. Europe—Economic
conditions—1945– 3. European Union. I. Title. II. Series.
HC240.H3136   1996
330.94—dc20   95–52583

Library of Congress Catalog Card Number: 95–52583
ISBN: 0–275–95582–6 Cloth
      0–275–95581–8 Paperback

Contents

Preface

This is a book about the disintegration of Europe. An astute observer pointed out to me that the title was a misnomer, since there never has been an integrated Europe as such. How true. And how precisely the remark puts the finger on the inherent difficulty that aspirations of greater union pose for Europe. By nature, it is a place of diversity.

Moreover, the rationale that justified the integration process appears to be wearing thin. Lasting peace in Europe will always remain a valid objective; the legitimacy of that aim can never be questioned. Yet the means, the framework, with which to approach that aim, can, over time, grow outmoded. Those days, when the immediate post-war leaders called upon Europe to unite, now lie on the other side of a deep divide that has opened up in history, between now and then, with the collapse of the cold war regime. The European Union is now like a troupe of trapeze artists deprived of both the safety net and the rope ladder that would lead them safely back to *terra firma*. How long before somebody misses a cue, or lets go altogether?

The problem is that economic forces are no longer at work that can pull the European peoples towards deeper integration. The reunification of Germany, welcome and glorious achievement as it is, has much to do with this state of affairs. And in the absence of a strong economic centripetal force, political argument alone cannot bring cohesion and indeed may lead to greater discord.

The origins of this book lie in an eight-part series on the same theme which was carried in the Japanese economic journal *The Mainichi Economist* in the spring of 1993. The series formed the basis of a book published in Japan by Nikkei Shimbun Publishers which came out in July 1994. *Disintegrating Europe* is the English language version of the Nikkei book with extensive updatings. The translations are my own.

None of these three attempts to write about Europe would have come remotely close to fruition without the guidance and the inspiration provided by Johsen Takahashi, a trusted and much admired senior colleague at the Mitsubishi Research Institute. I am very grateful to John Coleman, editor of *New European*, for his constant encouragement and his very great patience in spite of my having totally disillusioned him in regard to the mythical punctuality of the Japanese. Very many thanks are due to Joy Michaud for her careful and wise editing of the manuscript. I have learned a lot from her.

Noriko Hama

Prologue

Twilight of the Union

Richard Wagner's epic tetralogy *Der Ring des Nibelungen* opens with *Das Rheingold*, and ends in *Götterdämmerung*. As Europe enters its final stretch of the twentieth century, can the "European Construction" become for it the magical ring that ensures the coming of a golden future? Or will it prove to have been the Rheingold, the abuse of which dispatches the Gods to their fate in the twilight? What are the problems facing post-post-war, and post-"German"-unification Europe, as it tries to look beyond the dying embers of this century and into the dawn of the next?

"*Fatta l'Italia, dobbiamo fare gli italiani*"[1] (Having made Italy, we must now make Italians): thus spoke Massimo Taparelli d'Azelio as the unified Italian state was established in 1861. He spoke aptly, for though unification of the nation had indeed been realised, barely 10 per cent of the population were familiar with the standard national language. Given the circumstances, it was hardly to be expected that the people should immediately and of their own accord develop a strong sense of nationhood. Having made Italy, the founding fathers had now to set about the far more tortuous task of giving it a content, of nurturing the awareness of an Italian national identity, where no such notion had previously existed. The charismatic aura that had developed around Vittorio Emanuele II had to be employed to the full to achieve this goal.

A hundred and thirty-odd years later, on 1 November 1993, the Treaty on European Union, better known as the Maastricht Treaty, took effect and the European Community was renamed the European Union. On that day, could it have been the thoughts of Jacques Delors, the indefatigable champion of the European Construction, that having made Europe he now had to create Europeans? However, to assume he considered Europe a *fait accompli* is surely an insult to his obviously formidable intelligence. Lesser men than he would have been aware of the frail state of European unity, the increasingly apparent cracks in the structure. As for the making of Europeans, it looks to be a feat that requires all the centripetal magnetism of a modern-day Vittorio Emanuele combined with the strongest and most incontestable of tangible benefits that lends legitimacy to the notion of a single European identity.

Of how much substance can the European Union boast today? Very little, would appear to be the answer to this writer's alien eye. The Exchange Rate Mechanism of the European Monetary System, which was supposed to ensure stable currency relationships and, thus, pave the way towards eventual monetary union, is now but a caricature of its former self. The single market with its 340 million consumers, rather than being the source of renewed growth and wealth creation, became the place where an unprecedented 20 million unemployed Europeans had to roam in uncertainty. The Franco-German axis, once thought to be the unbreakable bond around which the European Construction would come to flourish, has begun to feel the corrosive effect of time and its hinges are now apt to creak in public.

A familiar argument is that all will be well once economic recovery is well under way. Another is that exchange rates are now so stable that, regardless of the effective demise of the ERM, the foundations of monetary union are now firmly in place.

The recovery does indeed seem to have arrived. Even the worst recession in post-war Europe cannot go on forever. Yet the crucial economic test for the European Union is not whether there is a recovery, but how strong a recovery it can deliver by virtue of closer integration. Can being an integrated area actually ensure greater growth momentum than would otherwise be the case? Can this be so, even when the constituent economies lack self-sustaining abilities of their own to generate incomes and employment? Moreover, it has to be remembered that West Germany, whose economic resilience was enough to cater for the rest of Europe, is now no more. It will be clear to any serious observer that the unified German economy cannot be expected to perform the same function. In the absence of the German growth engine, can it be convincingly argued that greater economic well-being is an intrinsic merit that deeper European integration promises?

To say that exchange rates are now stable, is merely a description of prevailing circumstances. It cannot explain away the underlying tensions which threaten to erupt at any time. The mere fact of temporary reprieve in the foreign exchange markets is a feeble basis on which to structure a single currency regime. To the extent that *franc fort* remains at the core of French monetary policy, the danger of self-strangulation is a constant threat that France must resign itself to. That masochism will always be a burden on Bundesbank monetary management.

At the December 1993 European Council meeting held in Brussels, the European Commission tabled a White Paper entitled *Growth, Competitiveness and Employment*. The much talked of document was to point the way out of the recessionary quagmire. Briefly, its prescription was twofold: firstly, a Marshall Plan-like spending programme to construct trans-European networks of roads, communication and energy supply; and secondly, a call for concerted effort to revive competitiveness through a better functioning labour market. Could this package be the all-resolving answer to Europe's difficulties?

Large-scale spending programmes that transcend national boundaries may, indeed, be effective as a provider of additional demand and new employment opportunity. The existence of a widespread network of basic infrastructures could lead to a better functioning single market. One would be hard put to argue against these points. Nonetheless, the Marshall Plan solution seems curiously out of step, if not out of date within the framework of late twentieth-century Europe. Is an economic area that is essentially comprised of economies well into their maturity capable of responding to such pump-priming measures without running into problems of capacity constraint? The prospects seem doubtful at best.

To be sure, there are member states within the EU which do not fall into the category of maturing economies, as such. For Greece, Portugal and Ireland, and perhaps to a lesser extent Spain, a modern-day Marshall Plan may not be such a bad idea. However, the question here would be the extent to which external resources could be counted on to provide capital and technological input.

Over and above these various points, it has to be remembered that what made the Marshall Plan so effective in post-war Europe was the presence of an immensely capital-abundant United States. Equally significant was the United States' determination to get Europe back on its feet, not least for its own purposes of market expansion and the deflection of spreading socialism. Europe did not have to worry about the financing. But today, the road back to growth and employment has to be self-funded. It is very seriously open to question whether the Community's member states, each struggling with their own over-spending problems, can collectively muster enough resources to generate the desired growth-enhancing effect without creating distortions elsewhere. What the trans-European infrastructure network idea amounts to is an attempt, through concerted action, to fill the growth gap that has been left as a result of lost (West) German expansionary momentum. While the need to fill that gap is indeed acute, there is, nonetheless, a considerable difference between the growth thrust produced by an economy riding high on a self-generated spiral of expansion and that which the combined efforts of maturing, and sometimes seriously ailing, economies can provide.

As for competitiveness, it is not a thing that can be planned and administered into existence. There is something inherently self-contradictory in the notion that states can get together and map out a course towards greater competitiveness. Competitiveness is surely something that is nurtured and fortified through the very act of competing against formidable opponents.

As many are quick to point out, wide swings between Euro-pessimism and Euro-euphoria have been a familiar feature of the European integration process. Thus, goes the conventional wisdom, the pendulum that is now poised at very much the Euro-pessimist extreme, will sooner or later have worked its way back to the opposite end of the arc. The Euro-gloom of the 1970s seemed all but to dispatch the Euro-enthusiasm of the '50s and '60s into total eclipse, only to be quickly forgotten as the following decade brought on the bubbly global boom and the dream of the single seamless European market. Is it not then reasonable to assume that the current disillusion with the European Construction will soon give way to a renewed sentiment of zeal and glowing expectation?

In response, it has to be asked whether Europe has ever before encountered, as it does today, such a fundamental transformation in the stage upon which it performs. Not only is the set design now completely altered, with the Iron Curtain no longer a part of the backdrop, but also one of the principal players has undergone a radical change of character, from a rich and politically silent West Germany into an economically troubled but more and more politically aware, if not ambitious, unified Germany. To all intents and purposes, it is an altogether different show that the Community now finds itself engaged in. The crisis of identity has never before appeared quite so profound as it does today.

As such, the challenge, not to say the threat, that the current situation poses for European integration surely belongs on an entirely different plane to that which gave birth to the Euro-pessimism of the 1970s. As tumultuous as those years were, they were still acted out within the framework of the post-war stage design. By the same token, a revival of popular enthusiasm for the European Construction will need something more than the Reaganomics/Thatcherism/Japanese bubble economy-induced illusion of world-wide well-being that was typical of the 1980s.

Towards the end of 1993, as the final stages of the Maastricht Treaty's ratification process was being fought over, something of a nostalgic longing for bygone days seemed to permeate through Europe. "Back to Basics" were the words that John Major sent forth from his podium at the British Conservative Party's annual party conference in October 1993. By so saying, he had launched a campaign for a return to traditional values and good old common sense: the basics on which British Conservatism stands.

The appeal was the Prime Minister's attempt to halt the alarming degree of public disenchantment and declining morale that had assailed the Tory Party over the preceding months. Internal feuds and schisms over Europe were a prominent cause of the Party's difficulties. Something had to be done to lift spirits and rekindle confidence. Thus the call to remember how decent and upright the British way of doing things used to be. The woeful plight of this particular campaign has been well-documented, not least in the tabloid papers. A series of colourful scandals involving Tory parliamentarians rapidly made a mockery out of traditional values and staunch conservatism, making "Back to Basics" one of the worst of the many disasters that have come John Major's way.

Ill-fated as it was, "Back to Basics" was not without kindred spirit. Just over a month before the Tory party conference in Britain, German Chancellor Helmut Kohl was urging his own people to recall their immediate post-war spirit of zest and enthusiasm. The post-unification economic malaise of the new German nation was deep. The people of western Germany, so used to being well-paid and well-protected within an environment of ever-shorter working hours, had grown progressively unhappy with the altered economic scenery. Citizens of the new eastern *Länder* were no less disillusioned, as ultra-high rates of unemployment continued to plague them. The initial, euphoria of a people reunited was rapidly turning sour.

For the grievances to be resolved, and for the nation to regain its erstwhile resilience, Germans needed to remember the way they once were. That was Mr Kohl's message. Where have those Germans gone, said he, who made possible Germany's post-war economic miracle and subsequent ascendancy up the ladder of international competitiveness? The Chancellor's plea to the public began with the complaint that Germany now had the oldest students, the youngest pensioners and the most idle machines in Europe. He, too, wished to see traditional values of hard work and self-sacrifice back in fashion.

No doubt Jacques Delors also, would have liked to see a bit of "Back to Basics" taking place among the member states of today's European Union. How much would he have welcomed a revival of the spirit of those early days, when there was so much enthusiasm for greater integration, such total determination to unite, so that great wars could never again break out on European soil?

Yet the mere going back to what once were the basics in times past seems hardly appropriate to today's historical setting. In the twilight of the twentieth century, the gods who envisioned the Valhalla of integrated Europe and their reasoning appear to be losing their contemporary relevance. Surely the new century calls for a new edifice, not shaped by the gods whose powers were destined to wane as the world grew out of its Cold-War framework and began to sail in untested waters. These are waters in which unified Germany struggles to come to terms with unfamiliar economic incompetence, while beginning tentatively to rediscover nationhood and political self-assertiveness; waters in which the current runs counter to the convergence of economic performance and policy management, thus making the attainment of a single currency regime a distant dream at best; rapid waters which large vessels with elaborate operation procedures may find difficult to negotiate. New ideas for a new age. The birth of new heroes is awaited as Europe attempts to journey beyond *Götterdämmerung*.

---

[1] Robert D. Putnam. *Making Democracy Work – Civic Traditions in Modern Italy*. Princeton. 1993

1

Turn-of-the-Century Europe

The Changing Economic Landscape in Britain, Germany and France

Towards the end of the 1980s and the early 1990s, the major European economies encountered many difficulties. Some of those difficulties were cyclical, but for the most part, they were structural ailments brought about, or forced out into the open, as a result of the very fundamental changes that assaulted those nations, individually as well as collectively. Their plights were the result of problems arising in the European integration process, but they in their turn became the cause of much disarray and conflict within the European Union. The turn-of-the-century European landscape is one fraught with turbulence.

1–1 Britain: Senior Citizen Tries to Run Too Fast

Annus Horribilis

As the world's oldest capitalist nation, the image of twilight well befits Britain. On 24 November 1992, at a Lord Mayor's banquet in honour of her fortieth anniversary on the throne, a somewhat bemused Queen Elizabeth II spoke of the year as having been an *annus horribilis* for her; a pun on the seventeenth-century poet and playwright John Dryden's *annus mirabilis*.

The year so far had indeed been plagued with one misfortune after another for Her Majesty: a series of marital problems within her own family, the partial burning down of Windsor Castle which triggered off a none-too-dignified row over whether or not the costs of its restoration should be met by public funds. This in turn led to a renewed argument regarding the question of whether or not the Queen ought to pay taxes.

Public sentiment at the time was largely sympathetic to the Queen's predicament. It did all seem a dismal enough way to celebrate forty solid years as reigning monarch. Yet the allusion to *"annus horribilis"* did elicit some negative response. For in the winter of 1992, there were not a few in Britain who felt that if anyone were to complain of a miserable year, it should be themselves rather than their sovereign. The prolonged recession had deprived people of jobs, and even of their homes, in the increasingly frequent instances of repossession. It was not altogether surprising under the circumstances that some among the Queen's subjects should find it unfeeling of her to grumble publicly over her private affairs.

The longest post-war recession on record had certainly cast deep gloom, not only on the economy as a whole but on aspects of people's everyday lives. Violent crime was on the ascendant, the homeless became a familiar feature on the streets of London, and frustration mounted against a Government seemingly powerless to remedy the situation. A Gallup poll conducted in February 1993 indicated that no less than 49 per cent of those surveyed wished to emigrate.

The level of unemployment that the recession generated was certainly one very acute cause of this proliferation of "anywhere but Britain" sentiment. As the Queen's *annus horribilis* speech was being delivered, the total number of the jobless in the country had reached 2.9 million. Speculation over exactly when the dreaded three million line would be reached had become a fashionable topic of conversation. The 1985-86 period was the only time in post-war history that British unemployment figures had tested those levels. The only other occasion was during the depth of the 1930s depression, when the number reached 3.4 million. Little wonder that the notion of 3 million on the dole should send unpleasant chills down the public's spine. That nightmare became reality in February 1993, when figures for January were released to show that a total 3.06 million people (before seasonal adjustment) had been registered as unemployed in that month. On 18 February, when the figures where made public, some 2,000 demonstrators gathered in Westminster to express their indignation against the Government's inability to contain the situation.

The Bubble Economy British-Style

On top of well-nigh the worst ever unemployment, the British people were penalised heavily for the over-borrowing and excess spending of the 1980s. The latter 1980s saw Britain involved in an unprecedented bout of credit expansion and asset inflation. During the 1985–90 period, bank credit (building societies included) grew by 20.3 per cent per annum, while property prices recorded a staggering 30 per cent annualised growth rate in 1988. Of such stuff was the British version of the bubble economy made. What followed in the 1990s was an inevitable process of unwinding, without which there was no hope of the economy ever regaining any semblance of equilibrium.

The building-up of the bubble economy *à la* Britain followed much the same process as it did in Japan and elsewhere. It was essentially one aspect of a global phenomenon that had resulted from successive years of United States overspending and its preoccupation with growth at any price. That said, the British bubble did have two distinct features all of its own. One was the effect of a depreciating currency through the 1985 to 1986 period. The other was the fact that over-borrowing was, by and large, concentrated in the household sector of the economy.

During the course of the 1980s, British households became the most heavily indebted of their kind among the industrialised economies. OECD statistics show Britain's ratio of household debts outstanding measured against nominal disposable income rising from 0.57 in 1980 to 1.00 in 1987, subsequently reaching 1.15 in 1991. Over the same 1980–1991 period, that ratio rose from 0.77 to 1.17 in Japan, and from 0.78 to 1.03 in the United States; neither of them small changes, but still falling well short of the British record.

Such accumulation of debts gave rise to even more dramatic changes in household savings ratios. Measured on a gross savings basis, the ratio toppled from its 1980 level of 13.3 per cent to a mere 5.6 per cent in 1988. Not even the United States, whose over-leveraged consumer spending and dwindling savings became a global subject of concern, was able to match this precipitous decline. There, the fall had been from a peak of 9.1 per cent in 1981 to 4.1 per cent in 1989.

Meanwhile, the value of the British household sector's real asset holdings bulged from 2.97 times its nominal disposable income in 1980 to 4.06 times the same in 1988. This was very much on a par with Japan, that most bubble-infected of economies, where the same ratio rose from 3.80 in 1980 to 6.31 in 1990. Needless to say, soaring property values were the principal driving force behind these developments in both countries.

Given the traditionally high rates of home-ownership in Britain, all this ballooning of asset values was bound to blunt people's aversion to debt accumulation. Meanwhile, lending institutions were scrambling to outdo each other as providers of cheap money in the wake of financial deregulation. The stage was set for the British households' descent into debtors' paradise.

Having, thus, become the centrepiece of the bubble economy, the household sector had inevitably to bear the brunt of the subsequent unravelling process. Monetary policy shifted towards tightening in 1988 and households were suddenly confronted with their debt problems, which they could no longer rely on ever-rising asset values to resolve. Real estate prices started to plummet and, one after another, heavily mortgaged households began to see the value of their homes falling below their original purchase price. This problem of negative equity, which instantly threatened people with repossessions, became increasingly acute as 1992 progressed. It was most manifest in the hitherto relatively recession-immune south-eastern region of the country, where more than 20 per cent of mortgaged property suffered from the phenomenon; London and its environs, where bubble-generation yuppies thronged, had understandably become the worst casualty of the downturn.

Faced with this abrupt turn-around in their fortunes, households rapidly began to rein in their borrowing. The growth of loans taken out from financial institutions (excluding mortgages) slowed to a mere 5 per cent in early 1992, where only a short while ago the norm had been an annual growth rate of 20 per cent. No doubt the reluctance of lenders to supply additional credit had as much to do with this as did borrower retrenchment. In any event, household net borrowings shrunk from a peak of 14.2 billion pounds in 1988 to just 1.7 billion pounds in 1991, with a move to a net repayments position of some 1 billion pounds by early 1992. As a result, the household net savings ratio began to climb up from its low of 5 per cent and had reached 12.3 per cent by the third quarter of 1992: a rate comparable to that of the early 1980s, before all the trouble began. The British bubble economy had been flattened.

The aftermath of its demise continued to bear down heavily on households, with many an entire family made homeless as a result of repossessions. While it is difficult to put a figure on such casualties, it is perhaps relevant to mention that by the third quarter of 1992, the total number of repossessed houses had reached 69,000. It is reasonable to assume that quite a few of the families driven out of those houses did indeed have to join the ranks of the wandering homeless. The post-bubble recession had indeed dealt the British population a heavy blow. No wonder some of them resented the Queen's preoccupation with her own private misfortune.

Farewell ERM

The advent of spring did bring about a change for the better, however. The "green shoots of recovery" that had so mockingly eluded policy makers every time they referred to them, had at last condescended to put in an appearance, now that spring was well and truly in the air. As 1993 progressed, industrial production turned positive, consumer credit began to register noticeably larger rates of net expansion, new house sales rose to levels some 20 per cent above the previous year. And finally even the unemployment rate began trending downward. As sceptical as ever, economists began to debate furiously amongst themselves whether such evidence of apparent recovery was to be taken at face value.

Yet by this time there was nothing that even the most suspicious of them should have found particularly questionable in the sighting of a bit of green shoot. For even as households were grimly struggling through their post-bubble adjustment process, Government policy had turned decidedly expansionist. The decisive shift in policy came on 16 September 1992. This was the day on which Britain was forced out of the ERM, alternatively referred to as Black Wednesday or White Wednesday, depending on people's perceptions of the impact that this event has had on the British economy.

Whichever perspective one chooses to adopt, the fact remains that with the departure from the ERM, John Major's Government had, to all intents and purposes, declared a *volte face* in economic management. So long as it remained a member of the ERM, the pledge to keep the pound's exchange rate within a 6 per cent band of fluctuation on either side of its 2.95 D-Mark ERM parity provided the British economy with a safeguard against growth-at-any-price extravagance. In May 1991, the then Chancellor of the Exchequer, Norman Lamont, had declared unemployment a price well worth paying for the containment of inflation. The Prime Minister himself had resolutely opined that "if it isn't hurting, it isn't working." Both appeared determined that monetary discipline and fiscal austerity should be the order of the day. That was then and this was now, however. The prolonged recession was just too much of a baptism of fire for them to retain their newly found faith in the ERM straitjacket. Time was now ripe to discard the suffocating garment.

In fairness, it has to be said that had Britain remained within the ERM at that particular point, domestic economic management could only have run into a dead end. Base rates in Britain stood at 10 per cent at the time, with only a 0.25 percentage point margin over the German Lombard rate. Had Britain dared to reduce rates further, there was very little hope of sterling remaining above the ERM floor of 2.78 D-Marks to the pound, let alone maintain the 2.95 D-Mark central rate. On the other hand, to halt the easing of monetary policy at this stage would have been nothing other than political suicide, when people were still losing not only jobs but their homes into the bargain. It was to be either the economy or the currency.

The only escape hatch out of this nightmarish trade-off was for the Germans to have lowered their interest rates. No such rescue was forthcoming, however, as Mr Lamont understandably grew increasingly more furious with Bundesbank intransigence. By the time the Germans finally did oblige with rate cuts, and this for reasons purely their own, sterling's fortunes were already beyond salvage.

Britain could, of course, have chosen to devalue without actually walking out of the ERM. But this would have made very little meaningful difference under the circumstances. The new parity would still have been difficult to maintain without a comfortable margin over German interest rates. Without a sustained fall in German rates, monetary freedom was a luxury Britain simply could not afford within the confines of the ERM, whatever the sterling's central rate. Freedom to pursue further monetary relaxation could only come with freedom from the straitjacket.

The Sweet Smell of Failure

Life after ERM was, indeed, freedom in motion for sterling. Its exchange rate against the D-Mark fell by more than 20 per cent from its previous central rate of 2.95 D-Marks to the pound. The fall *vis-a-vis* the yen and the dollar was even more dramatic, with rates falling to more or less 25 per cent below pre-Black Wednesday levels against the dollar and more than 35 per cent down against the yen.

Such drastic changes in exchange rate relationships were bound to make their effects felt on the domestic economy. Over the six month period following Black Wednesday, British exports registered a 19 per cent increase in volume terms. Exports to the rest of Europe declined by 1.6 per cent because of the recession there, but the fall would surely have been greater had it not been for the cheaper sterling. Still more noteworthy is the fact that imports from within the European Community declined by nearly 8 per cent over the same period. With the worst of the recession now over in Britain, the sharp drop was not attributable to a further shrinkage in domestic demand. Imports were being priced out of the British market due to the pound's depreciation. Given strong export growth and no competitive threats from imports, there was clearly more than a whiff of spring in the air for British manufacturers.

Without the straitjacket, domestic fiscal and monetary policies were also given considerably greater room for manoeuvre. As Norman Lamont announced immediately after Black Wednesday, the Government's economic policy would now pursue exclusively British interests, not European ones. True to the Chancellor's promise, base rates began to fall rapidly, eventually reaching 5.25 per cent by February 1994. Meanwhile, the 1992 Autumn Budget Statement was put forward with a "strategy for growth" as its central objective.

Low interest rates, a depreciating currency, go-for-growth public spending: these were the elements that constituted post-ERM British economic management. Unabashed expansionism had become the major thrust of policy. With all this going on, it would have been extraordinary had the economy not regained some growth momentum. A shrewd, but despairing, observer was quoted at the time as saying that what Britain needed was a set of policies suitable for a developing nation trying to take off, namely, cheap money, a low exchange rate, lavish public spending and import controls. Barring the last, this was precisely the policy mix adopted following Black Wednesday. And it seemed to work.

Yet Britain after all is, most emphatically, not a developing nation about to take off. What may indeed be a miracle cure for a nascent economy can only be devil's potion for the eldest member of the league of capitalist economies. Persisting on the growth-at-any-price course would have meant eventual collapse. Already pumped full of steroids over the bubble years, a further dose of the drug would surely have led to a cardiac arrest.

The 1980s were a decade, not only of asset inflation but also of the steady erosion of Britain's industrial base. As the chairman of GEC, Lord Prior, once lamented, "manufacturing industry is no longer there, and therefore, we have to source a lot of our components from other countries."[1] For such an economy, capacity constraints are never very far away. Too much demand pressure will all too soon rekindle inflation and lead to yet another nosedive into recession. The gyration between boom and bust has been a well-known constant feature of the British economy over the years.

Enter Kenneth Clarke

For the moment, policy seems set on avoiding a return to this roller coaster circuit. Contrary to the reputation that preceded him, the economic management of the current Chancellor of the Exchequer, Kenneth Clarke, has, thus far, not been that of a vote-grabbing politician going for growth at full throttle. Mr Clarke was seemingly not averse to tax increases and expenditure cuts, ruled out pre-election tax give-aways, and has not sanctioned public sector pay increases which were not accounted for by improvements in productivity. He surprised many with a prompt interest rate increase at the merest first flicker of revived inflationary pressure in September 1994. It has to be said that this latter move was largely seen to have as much to do with the increasing visibility and clout of the Bank of England as with Mr Clarke's monetary instincts. On the other hand, that strengthening of the Bank's position was at least in part due to Mr Clarke's decision to release minutes of his monthly meetings with the Bank's governor, Mr Eddie George.

Hitherto shrouded in a veil of secrecy, the debates behind interest rate manoeuvres have now become public property. It is no longer possible for the Chancellor to override the Bank's analysis without good and convincing economic reasoning. Used wisely and with integrity, this tool does have the potential of replacing the ERM as a straitjacket that protects the wearer as well as others from recurring fits of expansionist folly.

Much newsprint space has been devoted to speculation over the Chancellor's behaviour. Could it be that, incredible or otherwise, Mr Clarke was turning out to be one of the best Chancellors that Britain has had in recent years? Or are there political motives behind his moves, the intricacies of which have not been fathomed by observers? The answer is likely to be that he was merely following his political instincts and, being a shrewd politician, he arrived at the correct economic conclusion. It could well be that he was right for the wrong reasons. It may not always work.

As intriguing as this debate may be, the even more interesting and indeed more relevant question is where the economy itself is actually poised to go, as Mr Clarke presides over its management. How will the economy perform over the coming months and years? What is the position that it can hold in the vastly transformed and still changing landscape of today's Europe? What can a further integration of Europe, if that is to be the case, hold for the economy as it heads toward the twenty-first century? Alternatively, if the process of greater integration falters and fails, how will that affect the British economy?

Feeling Better?

The current state of the economy is in fact a curious one. The recovery has been in place for some time, real Gross Domestic Product is growing by rates well above 3 per cent, and prices are rising only very benignly with underlying inflation just a little more than 2 per cent. It looks as though the Government can justly boast of finally achieving that elusive goal of non-inflationary growth. And yet, this recovery has been labelled the "recovery without the feel-good factor." The warm glow of economic well-being is missing. People cannot feel the recovery. It has also been called a jobless recovery. While employment has been growing steadily, much of the incremental jobs have been part-time and low-paid. The employment opportunities that have come with this recovery have not been ones that thrill people. A "voteless recovery" in other words, as Tory Party Chairman, Jeremy Hanley, put it perceptively, if indiscreetly.

Joblessness and the absence of the feel-good factor are obviously strongly related. Not to mention those still on the dole, people with only temporary and inadequately-paid jobs do not experience a great deal of feel-good exhilaration. Hence, they do not go on a spending binge, at least, not on expensive luxury items. Bargain hunting has become something of a national exercise. This is very much the reason why prices have been so stable at the retail level. And this price stability itself is a factor that keeps the feel-good factor so hard to come by in spite of expanding production.

Something in the nature of a negative monetary illusion may be said to be at work here. In periods of high inflation, people are liable to bask in a sense of immense well-being, because nominal wages and asset values tend to rise very quickly. That sense of riches may be entirely false, since the real value of assets may have been thoroughly eroded by inflation, and real wages may actually be registering negative growth. Yet people are willing to spend in the belief that they are rapidly becoming very rich. This is precisely the kind of feel-good factor that has been missing from Britain's post-bubble recovery.

In theory, the rise in the real value of assets that results from stable prices should effect people's spending behaviour in the same way as does the sudden boost in nominal asset values caused by inflation. However the effects of an inflationary and a deflationary cycle are not symmetrical. This, in fact, is what the monetary illusion is all about. Moreover, debt burdens become heavier in times of disinflation. Thus, stable prices may not necessarily be of much help to those still many indebted households.

The situation is a tricky one. It may arguably be said that without the feel-good factor, a self-feeding expansion can never really get going. But if it is the case that the feel-good factor cannot be generated without monetary illusion, then price stability has to be sacrificed at the altar of go-for-growth expansionism, and the risk of a boom-bust cycle begins to loom large. A combination of ample spare capacity, very strong demand growth and rapid productivity increase is what is needed for the feel-good factor to permeate, even in the absence of inflation. These, however, are circumstances that do not readily co-exist in maturing industrial economies. Just as a policy mix of low interest rates, large-scale help from the Government and low exchange rates can only make sense over prolonged periods in the case of developing economies, a world of stable prices and rising production is not really an option that is open to ageing ones. For this to become a feasible option, an economy would need to undergo fundamental rejuvenation of a kind that is apt to involve profound social upheaval.

It should also be noted that stability of price indices *per se* does not necessarily imply the existence of spare capacity. Where suppliers are sacrificing profitability in order to maintain sales volume, the macroeconomic supply constraints may actually be mounting and inflationary pressures rising without any outward sign that this is happening. This may well be the case in an economy where "manufacturing industry is no longer there."

If awareness of this problem was what lay behind Mr Clarke's seemingly pre-emptive rate increase, his caution is certainly to be commended. Yet insofar as that caution is given priority, the feel-good factor may forever elude him. On the other hand, if the superficial stability of prices tempts or induces him to hold back on further early tightening, pent-up inflationary pressures may burst forth in full force at some point, leading once more into the dreaded boom-bust cycle.

The upshot of all this, is that for this most senior of Europe's capitalist citizens, there is little room for manoeuvre. The choice seems to be confined to either prolonged periods of anaemic growth that create neither adequate jobs nor sufficient profitability, or repetitive boom-bust swings that leave the economy increasingly more exhausted at the end of each business cycle.

What can being a part of an "ever closer union" of European nations mean for such an economy? That it could not tolerate the discipline of the exchange rate straitjacket has already been demonstrated. The single market does continue to have its attractions. However, for an economy with limited capacity, trying to serve both the domestic and European markets at the same time, it may become just too costly in terms of inflation. Moreover, the question is whether Britain is capable of maintaining sufficient inroads into the single market without the fiercely competitive exchange rate position that it has carved out for itself, following its departure from the ERM. In an interview with the Independent, John Major once made the point that ". . . we are penetrating deep into the German market in a way we never did before."[2] This was in early 1993, when recovery of the German economy was as yet nowhere in sight. With this in mind, Mr Major further went on to say, "even though their market has temporarily shrunk, we are establishing a foothold in it of a sort we did not get."

Unlike his predecessor, Mr Major is the last person to whom predatory instincts seem readily attributable. Nevertheless, those remarks do in themselves imply a strategy of aggressive competitive devaluation, with the intent of biting off a large chunk of other people's markets even when they are not expanding. The traditional term for such a strategy is beggar-thy-neighbour policy. If this is the basis on which Britain has to trade with its counterparts on the European continent, it cannot be a very happy state of affairs for either side.

Subsequent developments suggest that the Queen may well have been premature in naming just the year 1992 as her one *annus horribilis*. The mud-slinging within her immediate family seems simply to go from bad to worse. While things do not seem quite so hopeless for the nation over which she reigns, nor do a series of *anni mirabiles* appear within easy reach.

1–2 Germany: Which Way Out of the Unification Trap?

On 16 October 1994, Chancellor Helmut Kohl's ruling coalition was re-elected into the German Bundestag, albeit with a wafer-thin majority. At that point, Mr Kohl had been leader of his party, the CDU, for twenty-one years, and German Chancellor for twelve. By 1998, when the next general election is due, he will have become the longest-serving Chancellor in post-war German history. He will only need until 1996 to match Konrad Adenauer's fourteen years in office in former West Germany. Thus, it looks as though Mr Kohl is about to have his cake and eat it too. He is now poised to go down in history as the father of unified Germany and the forger of a united Europe. What more could he ask for?

Yet at this juncture, making those two things go hand-in-hand does not look easy. Is the concept of a united Europe actually compatible with the existence of a unified Germany? What kind of a European Union is it that is acceptable to today's Germany? Can a unified Germany blend comfortably into a European Union, whose original design did not assume its rebirth?

Collective Gloom

An economic perspective on Germany needs to question whether what made sense for pre-unification West Germany continues to make sense for unified Germany: whether or not unified Germany can continue to play the same economic role that West Germany played for Europe in the days when the Wall was still standing.

"We have the oldest students, the youngest pensioners and the most idle machines"[3]: not the lamentation of a frustrated British industrialist, but the words of Helmut Kohl, uttered in September 1993. Election victory and a cyclical pickup in the economy may have since lifted the gloom a little, but much of the cause of his dissatisfaction remains intact today.

Once the undisputed economic champions of Europe, Germans suddenly appeared to lose much of their self-esteem following reunification. Not a day would pass without an industrialist or two bewailing the low morale of his workforce, the rise in absenteeism, the heavy burden of welfare contributions, regulatory constraints, and inflexible unions. The unions in their turn accused management of treachery, of undermining the *Soziale Marktwirtschaft*. The traumas of unification and the deepest recession in fifty years made the post-war German economic miracle seem like a distant dream. A sense of insecurity pervaded the unions, making them militant and suspicious, and management responded with fretful disdain.

The state of collective depression was at its deepest when those complaints of Chancellor Kohl's were uttered. His words were by way of being the preamble to a discussion paper entitled "Securing the Future of Germany's Economic Base," which the Economics Ministry had put forward. What the document amounts to is a comprehensive list of the problems that lie behind the Chancellor's words and the remedies needed to cure the economy of the malaise.

The report's content and arguments are by now familiar ground. It criticises German workers for expecting too much from business and the Government. It says there is too much state intervention and excessive regulation, structurally depressed industries are given too much help and not enough money goes into the development of the nation's technological infrastructure. A total overhaul of the existing system is necessary, involving massive privatisation and deregulation, welfare reform, education reform, more flexible employment practice, longer working hours, less of the guild-like division of labour among workers, and more competition. Through all this, the report hopes that the hardworking, tenacious spirit, which once made Germany so great, may be revived.

That the paper's indictments are legitimate is uncontested. In fact, the problems identified in the paper are not new. They have been recognised as symptomatic of the "German disease" since the early 1970s. Yet so long as the growth machine was functioning smoothly, the pampered society was allowed to keep on basking in its glory; "give me chastity and continency – but not yet." The significance of the Bonn Government's report lay in its message that it was no longer possible to put off the day of reckoning. The conversion had to take place today, or else damnation. Reunification had driven in stoppers and the cogwheels of the growth machine had been thrown out of action.

Too Much Equality Too Soon

Since reunification, western Germany has been providing its brethren in the eastern *Länder* with funds equivalent to roughly 5 per cent total GDP. It is simply not possible to maintain such massive levels of income transfer and still keep the welfare state going as though nothing had changed. The social market economy may still have been sustainable within the framework of the pre-unification *Bundesrepublik*. Chastity could still have waited for another day. But taking eastern Germany on board as well, when there was already trouble brewing nearer home, has made the whole state of affairs much too costly for comfort.

The West German economy was about to reach the high point of an ongoing expansion when the Berlin Wall came down. Signs of overheating were already much in evidence. Under the circumstances, the upsurge in construction activity in eastern Germany, coupled with the zest of east German consumers, exposed for the first time to the allures of the market economy, could not have failed to lead to hyper-boom conditions. Thus, the seeds of all the ensuing difficulties were sown.

Meanwhile, policy had taken a bold if not reckless turn. A decision was made to introduce the Deutsche Mark into eastern Germany at an astronomically favourable conversion rate for the Ost Mark; 1-to-1 for wages and smaller savings deposits, 1-to-2 for larger accounts. The move swept away any possibility of an efficient division of labour taking place between the two Germanies. The actual purchasing power differential would have put the conversion rate at 1-to-7 or even 1-to-10. Had such realistic ratios been adopted, something on the lines of a mutually beneficial vertical division of labour may have been possible. Eastern Germany did not have the capital stock to match that of the west. But it would have been able to provide a large supply of cheap labour, taking some of the excessive heat out of the reunification boom.

Some observers did point out at the time that the introduction of cheap labour from the eastern *Länder* was the very thing that was needed to galvanise the increasingly inflexible labour market in western Germany. This would lead to a generally more competitive and efficient wage structure, providing a way out of the sclerosis that had so alarmed Chancellor Kohl. Injection of new blood is certainly not a bad idea when lethargy and paralysis show signs of spreading. Reunification could indeed have provided at least some relief from the malaise discussed in the Economics Ministry study.

What actually occurred was precisely the reverse. Because of the near 1-for-1 currency conversion, unification meant yet more demand pressure on west German industries without any help on the supply side from the east. Karl Otto Pöhl, the then President of the Bundesbank, argued strongly against the folly of such a monetary union. But at the time, there was little room for economic concerns to temper the sense of political urgency pushing monetary union forward.

A different development may have emerged had workers in the east decided to offset the uncompetitive currency conversion rate by undercutting their own wages. This solution clearly did not appeal to the citizens of the eastern *Länder*, however. From day one, they wanted to avail themselves of the living standards of the West. Wage dumping was not for them.

Nor did organised labour in western Germany have any intention of allowing this to happen. The unions could not risk long established workers' rights and the hitherto impregnable cohesion of their members being thrown into jeopardy by unbridled competition from their brothers in the east. In a pre-emptive move, west German trade unions declared "social solidarity," calling for prompt wage equalisation between the two Germanies. East German workers had no reason to object. West German businesses were all too willing to lend support, since rapid wage parity would have meant less threat of low-cost competition from their counterparts in the east. East German companies did not know enough about market forces to protest. So it was that, in March 1991, all three parties agreed to aim for wage equalisation by 1994.

Nothing could have been more out of touch with reality given the difference in productivity that existed between east and west. East German industrial productivity was not much more than one-third of that of western Germany at the time. It was clearly outrageous to assume that this yawning gap could be eliminated within the space of three years. As subsequent events have demonstrated only too well, going ahead with the wage equalisation plan was bound to have disastrous effects on the macroeconomic balance of unified Germany. Western Germany had missed out on a golden opportunity to perform invigorating surgery on its sclerotic labour market and the cost structure of its businesses. East German workers for their part were on the way to pricing themselves out of a potentially sizeable market for their skills.

From Boom to Bust

As the unification boom took off, west German workers demanded ever higher wages, which businesses could ill afford to reject, given the market pressures they themselves were facing. Pay settlement levels soared in the west, and those surging levels became the target of the wage equalisation plan for the east. As a result, average monthly wages per employee in eastern Germany rose by 72.1 per cent between the third quarter of 1990 and the fourth quarter of 1991. Meanwhile, production as measured by real GDP had declined by a hefty 14.2 per cent in the eastern *Länder*. Something clearly had to give, and employment went hurtling down in the east, shrinking by 18.7 per cent over the same time period.

Urgent support was needed for the suddenly massive pool of redundant workers, and relief also had to be provided for east German businesses, if that pool was to be prevented from getting too large too quickly. Transfer payments from western German began to snowball. With expenditure on infrastructure construction already bulging on the one hand, it did not take long for post-unification income transfers to drive the German public sector into deficit.

Not surprisingly, the Bundesbank did not intend to allow either fiscal laxity or rapid wage increases to lead to runaway inflation. Interest rates began to rise, dealing an added blow to west German businesses already suffering from the higher wage cost pressures. This led to further profit declines, lower investments and still more manpower cuts. The unification bubble was about to burst and recessionary gloom was waiting just around the corner.

The situation took a noticeable turn for the worse in the autumn months of 1991. The third and fourth quarters of 1991 both registered negative GDP growth rates in western Germany. The first quarter of 1992 was helped by a warm winter which resulted in strong construction activity. This, however, soon gave way to a general weakness, with zero growth rate in the second quarter, followed by negative growth rates again in the third and fourth quarters. Growth rate for the year came in at 1.5 per cent; a sharp slowdown from 3.7 per cent in 1991. For 1993, GDP growth registered a negative 1.7 per cent and pan-German unemployment reached 3.5 million. When all those workers nominally employed in eastern Germany on short-time work schedules and government sponsored job-creating programmes were taken into account, unified Germany now had effectively five million unemployed people, with more than one-third of them out of work for more than one year. The economic downturn in western Germany drove public sector budgets further into the red, and the once exemplary state of the nation's finances deteriorated rapidly.

The recession is now over. But the structural problems in eastern Germany remain. So does the need to compensate for them through income transfers from western Germany. Western Germany is, therefore, under pressure to deliver persistently higher and potentially inflationary growth rates. None of the basic distortions that were caused by unification has been resolved fundamentally. As the Bundesbank is right to caution, improving growth prospects of the moment should not be allowed to deter the Bonn Government from addressing itself to the more deep-rooted economic and social disequilibria that are still in place. These were the factors that drove Germany into its worst post-war recession; it was not the recession that created those problems.

Reunification was a major transplant operation which would have brought on complications even if a meticulous matching of the relevant organs had been conducted prior to surgery. No such compatibility existed between the two Germanies and yet they were sewn together as though they were a perfect match, as if sharing a common currency and common wage levels would suit both sides admirably. Under the circumstances it was unthinkable that serious distortions would not ensue, and it will now take time for the stitch marks to disappear completely.

Social Partners in Conflict

The hasty wage equalisation pact not only did not work, but also had the added effect of driving a wedge into Germany's traditional consensus society. Utopian harmony is not an easy thing to maintain when there is no longer enough to provide for everyone. All the more so when, in spite of the income shortfall, share and share alike still has to be the governing principle.

The first revolt against consensus came from the management camp. According to the wage pact, steel industry workers in eastern Germany were to have been given a pay rise of 26 per cent in April 1993. A similar agreement was also in place for the non-ferrous metals and electrical industries, where the scheduled wage increase was 21 per cent. When it came to the day, however, the management side simply refused to let this happen. They proposed instead that east German wages be raised by 9 per cent, which was roughly in line with the rate of inflation in eastern Germany at the time. The unions were enraged and threatened to retaliate with a general strike. For the first time in post-war history, the social partners were headed for a genuine confrontation.

Moreover, the problem did not stop there, for even as the labour-management rapport was rapidly unravelling, both sides were beginning to experience a breakdown of solidarity among their own members. On the management side, companies with production sites located in the eastern *Länder* were in search of a compromise, notwithstanding the 9 per cent hard-line offer being tabled by their leaders. Some were willing to raise wages as planned for the month of April, and renegotiate the deal for subsequent months. Others would go along with the original agreement for 1993, if the unions were willing to compromise on the timing of full wage equalisation. The unions for their part, were also encountering dissent among their ranks in the east. Headstrong pursuit of wage equalisation was beginning to be regarded as doing more to kill off jobs than to lead to larger incomes.

In the end, the dispute was resolved by pushing back the target year for wage equalisation to 1996. It was also agreed that loss-making companies should be exempted from the wage pact. The compromise prevented an all-out confrontation, but hardly amounted to a full restoration of mutual goodwill. Judgement day had been put off for a mere two years and the rifts and cracks that had appeared between labour and management, between east and west, were not about to melt away.

Meanwhile, social intolerance of a different, but not unrelated kind, had begun to emerge. Violence against immigrant workers and the proliferation of neo-Nazi activity became a worrisome feature of unified German society. While German voters sensibly turned their backs on the ultra-right movement in the October 1994 general election, social discontent manifested itself in another form. On that occasion, it was not to the far right but in the opposite direction that the disgruntled public chose to turn. The Party of Democratic Socialism (PDS), formerly the Communist Party of East Germany, won 4.4 per cent of the total vote, entitling them to thirty seats in the Bundestag under the complex German electoral system.

Support for the PDS was overwhelmingly concentrated in eastern Germany. More than 19 per cent of the votes cast in the five new *Länder* went to them, while in the west they captured only a minuscule 0.9 per cent of the votes. To its supporters, the PDS had come to be the voice for eastern Germany. Its election campaign was a well targeted one. The east German people were reminded of the social stability, job security, and the sense of solidarity which had existed prior to unification. The east German identity was stressed, and promises were made that that identity would be championed forcefully by the PDS in the Bundestag. Economic hardship and a sense of waning social integrity, the two negative winds of change that east Germans had felt most exposed to, had been focused on to much effect.

Back to a Future of the Command Economy?

The Bonn Government has been at great pains to pull the nation together, to pave over the cracks in the social fabric of unified Germany. Yet the harder it has tried, the more it seems only to have succeeded in enhancing the interventionist nature of German society. Unification was supposed to bring eastern Germany into the market economy, thereby opening up a window of opportunity for its citizens through which they could reach out and grasp prosperity. But in actual fact, it looks as though the pull has worked more in the other direction, with western Germany being gradually sucked into the black hole of more planning, more controls, and more Government intervention.

Take, for instance, Chancellor Kohl's call for a "solidarity pact" between Government, business and labour to tackle the post-unification traumas in unison. The federal Government would continue vigorously to support reconstruction in the east, while enlisting the support of local governments as well as the opposition parties, to cut back the budget deficit. Businesses would ensure a steady flow of private capital into eastern Germany through investments, lending, and procurement. Unions would restrain their wage demands. All for one and one for all. Only through such solidarity could a steady path towards greater prosperity be restored.

There is nothing to be said against the spirit of the proposal. Yet the idea that a grand coalition of all the forces concerned should purposely and single-mindedly work towards a common goal sounds like something out of the textbooks of a socialist nation running a command economy. Solidarity of purpose can certainly lead to results. But on the other hand, it does not take that large a step to move from a request for wage moderation to the imposition of mandatory wage and price controls. Capital does need to flow from west to east, but the east will forever be a bottomless pit if the solidarity pact is the only basis on which the flow of capital can be maintained. Too much management and control will lead to waning growth momentum, and however much solidarity is brought to bear, an economy will not be able to distribute more income than it is capable of generating.

The Devaluation Alternative

That ability to deliver sufficient income growth will be one of the key policy issues for Mr Kohl as he sets about becoming the longest-serving German Chancellor in post-war history. The task will not be easy. Industries in western Germany have learned their lesson well. Mindful of their high cost thresholds and declining competitiveness, they have been restructuring with great determination. Their efforts will eventually bear fruit, if they have not already begun to do so. But their success will not necessarily mean a return to resilience at the macroeconomic level, since what restructuring amounts to is labour shedding, progressive out-sourcing and more offshore production.

The more German companies achieve in cost-cutting, the less income they will be liable to generate within the confines of the domestic economy. The best companies may thrive, but their achievements will not ensure greater wealth for the national economy. Far from solidarity, what companies will be seeking is to break free from the rigidities and costliness involved in doing business at home. In the kind of circumstances that Germany finds itself today, its macroeconomic performance may not correspond to a sum of its microeconomic parts. Yet this decoupling cannot be allowed to happen if eastern Germany is not to degenerate into a permanent disaster area, constantly in need of Government-orchestrated assistance.

One quick-fix way to prevent an exodus of west German industries out of their homeland would be to devalue the D-Mark. Given a cheaper D-Mark, companies would lose the incentive to move production and procurement offshore. Improved export prospects could lead to more hiring of people at home. That a competitive exchange rate provides a short cut to faster growth has been well illustrated by the British and Italian experience following their departure from the ERM. The temptation to go the same route cannot be small for today's Germany.

It may be blasphemy to associate such thoughts with an economy presided over by the Bundesbank, and it goes without saying that a stable currency is one of the most fundamental underpinnings of a healthy economy. But can that maxim remain as unshakeable for unified Germany as it had been for West Germany? It cannot be just coincidence that complaints from the German business community about an over-valued D-Mark have increased noticeably since unification.

Having been returned to power by the thinnest of thin majorities, Mr Kohl will find it more difficult than ever to impose painful adjustments on the nation. Despite all his calls for a return to the immediate post-war spirit of self-sacrifice and diligence, the Chancellor may begin increasingly to consider a weaker D-Mark as the less politically hazardous alternative. Suspend for a moment the belief that the Bundesbank would never sanction such a move, and it should not come as that much of a surprise to see Germany pursuing the cheaper D-Mark option. There are times when even the most relentless custodians of price stability have to yield to changes in the economic environment.

Life was hard enough for the other EU states when they had to maintain high interest rates so as to keep pace with the strong D-Mark. The situation could grow even more difficult if Germany were indeed to switch to a weaker D-Mark policy. A Germany engaged in competitive devaluation is not a happy thought. But it could happen if no alternative routes can be found to lead Germany back to macroeconomic equilibrium.

Looking Eastward

One possible alternative is for Germany to look east; to build a D-Mark zone that extends eastwards into Central and Eastern Europe. If macroeconomic equilibrium is not sustainable within the closed circuit of unified Germany itself, a wider plain has to be sought. More specifically, a sphere of activity has to be secured for eastern Germany, so that it need not continue to depend on perpetual income transfers from the west. Once the supreme performer among COMECOM nations, the best economic medicine for eastern Germany would be to start making its own living once more. Mr Kohl's enthusiasm for the EU's eastward enlargement implies that this may be the way his mind is working.

The scenario is not without its risks. Quite apart from the political tensions involved, eastward expansion could prove self-defeating from a purely economic perspective, since eastern Germany could all too easily turn into a mere transit zone through which both capital and employment opportunity stampede across into Central and Eastern Europe. Moreover, there is always the possibility that the whole of

Central and Eastern Europe may turn into an infinitely more bottomless version of the five eastern *Länder*, needing ever larger flows of financial assistance from western Germany.

Notwithstanding these potential risks, the strengthening of economic ties with Central and Eastern Europe remains a key issue for German industrialists. Many advocate a vertical division of labour whereby their easterly neighbours would specialise in the production of basic manufactures, while both western and eastern Germany step incessantly up the ladder of higher value added production.

A Germany bent on the eastward extension of its sphere of influence may be even more anathema to the rest of Europe than a Germany inclined to competitive devaluation. Yet, given the circumstances, the incentive to forge eastward is strong. Germany's loyalty to the EU is being severely tested by its changing economic fortunes.

1–3 France: The *Franc Fort* Straitjacket

Balladur's Dash to Bonn

On 31 March 1993, a conservative coalition Government was formed in France for the first time in fifteen years. General elections held over the twentieth and twenty-eighth of the month had handed the alliance between the Gaulist RPR and Valéry Giscard d'Estaing's centre-right UDF a clear victory over the socialists. Thus, for a second time following the period 1986–88, the Fifth Republic was to be placed under the stewardship of a *cohabitation* between a socialist President and a conservative government.

The newly-appointed Prime Minister, Edouard Balladur, promptly chose Germany as his first port of call outside France. This was in itself hardly surprising given the intimacy of the Bonn-Paris axis, but the swiftness of the move was, nonetheless, significant. It was a reflection of the extent to which French economic management was hostage to German monetary policy at the time.

Inflation by then had ceased to be a problem in France. Consumer prices were rising by no more than 2 per cent in annual terms. Nevertheless, short term interest rates were still hovering above 10 per cent, because of the need to maintain an adequate premium over equivalent German rates. Otherwise, the franc would start to weaken against the D-Mark, and this the French could not allow. French businesses were compelled to endure punishingly high real interest rates of 8 and even 9 per cent, in order to ensure exchange rate stability. Smaller enterprises suffered the most due to their high degree of dependence on short term borrowing, but the larger businesses were by no means left unharmed. Business failures mounted and unemployment soared, topping three million with alarming speed.

The ailing economy soon made its difficulties felt on the national budget. Up to 1991, the French budget deficit had amounted to no more than a commendable 1 per cent of nominal GDP. But 1992 brought about a radical change in the situation with a 226.3 billion franc deficit, corresponding to 3.2 per cent of GDP. All the good work that had gone into improving the nation's finances had been undone at a stroke. One of the first things Mr Balladur had to do on taking office was to instruct his cabinet members to aim for a minimum 20 billion franc cut in overall national expenditure.

All this had come about because of the *franc fort* policy which dictated that the French franc should under no circumstances be devalued against the D-Mark. This meant that French interest rates could never come down while German rates remained high. Inherited from the previous Government, this policy was bringing undue deflationary pressure to bear on the French economy; a pressure that was becoming increasingly painful to endure as Mr Balladur came into power.

To the extent that the *franc fort* remained inviolable, there could be no relief for the French economy unless German interest rates were to come down. Under the circumstances, there was little else that Mr Balladur could do but to rush to Chancellor Kohl and plead his case. The other option of abandoning the *franc fort* policy was not really an option at all. France was not ready to stoop so low. And yet the very desire to not bow down before the D-Mark was driving the newly appointed French premier into running to the German Chancellor for help. The situation was becoming somewhat bizarre.

Bérégovoy Killed in Action

A shocking incident occurred, whilst Mr Balladur was busily engaged in putting together his economic policy and in relations-building with the German Chancellor: his Socialist predecessor, Pierre Bérégovoy, committed suicide on 1 May 1993. Mr Bérégovoy's motives for taking his own life are clearly nobody else's business. Nevertheless, the days leading up to the event cannot have been either very rewarding or uplifting for this seasoned politician, who was to draw the curtain on fifteen years of socialist rule in the Fifth Republic.

A trusted deputy of President Mitterrand, it was nonetheless very late in the day that Mr Bérégovoy was given the opportunity to head his own cabinet. It was only after the Socialist Party had suffered a resounding defeat in the April 1992 local elections that his turn came about. The controversy-prone Madame Edith Cresson having stepped down from the premiership at this point, it was left for Mr Bérégovoy to take over the all-but-defunct Socialist Government. Of the clearly raw deal that he had been treated to, Mr Bérégovoy was quoted as saying: "The President chose Fabius because he was the youngest, Rocard because he was the most brilliant, Cresson because she was a woman. Finally, he named me, when it was already too late."[4]

Subsequent developments must have been equally, if not more, frustrating for him. Mr Bérégovoy was a staunch guardian of the *franc fort* policy. He had defended the policy as Finance Minister in the previous Government and continued to do so after becoming Prime Minister. For this, he had continuously to expose the French economy to cripplingly high real interest rates. No other course was open to him without lower German rates. But the people hated him and his Government for the policy.

Having, thus, sacrificed his own political future at the altar of *franc fort*, what should Mr Bérégovoy see following the Kohl-Balladur meeting in Bonn, but a rapid turn around in the direction of his country's interest rates. In the month of April 1993 alone, the French standard market intervention rate was reduced four times, with other cuts to follow. Adding insult to injury, the franc showed no sign of losing value against the D-Mark in spite of the narrowing interest rate differential. Mr Bérégovoy had good reason to feel more than a little hurt and betrayed by the abandonment of the policy he had fought so hard and for so long to sustain.

A touch of post-election euphoria was no doubt a cause of the franc's apparent resilience. But more than anything, it was helped by a surprise decision by Germany to ease its own monetary policy. On 22 April, the very day when Mr Balladur was to see the German Chancellor, the Bundesbank moved to shave 0.25 points off its discount rate, as well as 0.5 points off the Lombard rate, bringing the two rates down to 7.25 per cent and 8.5 per cent respectively. The exact synchronisation with the Kohl-Balladur meeting may or may not have been intended. In any event, it would have required superhuman tolerance or insensitivity, or both, for Mr Bérégovoy to maintain his equanimity at this point. If German interest rates could come down now, why not earlier? It looked very much as though the long suffering socialist warrior had perished in the line of a thankless and wearing duty.

The Franc Under Fire

By comparison, the future looked considerably brighter for Mr Balladur's Government; it had achieved the coveted feat of easing monetary policy without compromising the franc's exchange rate against the D-Mark. The euphoria was not allowed to last for long, however; Edouard Balladur's first ordeal came only three months into his leadership.

Mr Balladur's Economics Minister, Edmond Alphandéry, was due to see his German counterpart, Theo Waigel, on 25 June 1993, for a session of the regular Franco-German economic and financial council meeting. This meeting, however, had to be postponed because of a last-minute pull-out by Mr Waigel, the German Finance Minister. The reason given for Mr Waigel's withdrawal was that he had his hands full with the 1994 budget. But this was obviously nothing more than a pretext, and there was little doubt it was intended to be understood as such. The French side had clearly incurred the German Finance Minister's displeasure.

The reported cause of the quarrel was a media performance by Mr Alphandéry. On the day before the scheduled meeting, he was heard on a radio programme with comments to the effect that he hoped for a swift reduction in German interest rates. This gave the impression that the scheduled meeting was to be held for the exclusive purpose of discussing a co-ordinated Franco-German easing of monetary policy. This the Germans found not at all to their liking. Barely a few hours after Mr Alphandéry's interview, came the German announcement that Mr Waigel had decided to absent himself from the bilateral meeting. Not content with merely giving his counterpart the cold shoulder, Mr Waigel subsequently went on to make his own radio broadcast, categorically denying that a co-ordinated rate cut was in the pipeline, and putting great stress on the independence of German monetary policy from any outside influence.

Faced with deepening recession and nonetheless stubborn inflationary pressure, German irritation with Mr Alphandéry's intervention was understandable. The federal Government and the Bundesbank were involved in an intricate war of nerves over whether it was the economy or currency stability that deserved pride of place in the circumstances.

The last thing they needed was for France to complicate matters with its unsolicited opinions.

The tone of Mr Alphandéry's utterances did not help, moreover. "We are going to speak as equal to equal . . . This was not the case a few months ago . . ." said he, going on to proclaim: "Today the franc can support itself, perhaps better than the D-Mark."[5] While the stability of the French franc since the start of the Balladur Government did lend support to his confidence, the German side could hardly be expected to take such defiance against Deutsche Mark supremacy lying down. The insult would be doubly intolerable, should the impression be allowed to spread that German policy-makers were actually being summoned to Paris by their counterparts to discuss interest rate manoeuvres. There was no choice but for Mr Waigel to make his indignation apparent.

In the event Mr Alphandéry did not even experience the satisfaction of having his pronouncements vindicated. It turned out to be more of a case of tempting fate, for barely three weeks had elapsed since his "the franc can support itself better than the D-Mark" remark, before the franc came under heavy attack from a tidal wave of currency speculation. The assault was triggered by a gloomy economic forecast prepared by INSEE, the French statistical office, which predicted a 0.7 per cent decline in GDP in 1993, with the unemployment rate reaching 12.5 per cent by the year-end.

Disliking the lacklustre outlook, and spurred by the prospect of a further lowering of French interest rates, the market's reaction was a violent one. Concentrated selling repeatedly dragged the franc down perilously close to its then D-Mark floor rate of 3.4305FF/DM. Persistent intervention was needed to prevent it falling below the psychologically important resistance level of 3.42FF/DM. Mr Alphandéry had been heavily penalised for his *faux pas*.

The franc recovered some ground towards mid-July, but this was just a brief respite before the real blow. Everything hinged, yet again, on the Bundesbank's move. Its last council meeting before the summer recess was due on 29 July. Whether or not it would decide to lower interest rates on that occasion was the critical question. If it did cut rates, this would be a sign that there was still some life left in Franco-German policy co-ordination. If it did not, the franc's fate was sealed.

As the markets watched in fascination, the Bundesbank went teasingly halfway. Of the two interest rates under Bundesbank command, the Lombard rate was reduced by a full percentage point to

7.75 per cent, but the discount rate was left unchanged. Yet a discount rate cut was in fact what Prime Minister Balladur and his Economics Minister were waiting for. A widening of the differential between the German discount rate and the French intervention rate would have given the franc some additional breathing space. Realising that the Bundesbank had chosen to turn its back on the franc, the markets resumed their attack on the currency with a vengeance. Soon other currencies were sucked into the speculative maelstrom and eventually the whole of the ERM became embroiled in the turmoil. It was clearly becoming impossible to contain the situation through intervention alone, and an emergency meeting of finance ministers and central bank governors was convened to discuss the appropriate course of action.

The outcome of those talks was the wider band. As of 2 August 1993, the ERM would move from its original 2.25 per cent margin of allowable fluctuation on each side of the ECU parity, to a band of 15 per cent each way. With such a vastly widened range of freedom, the ERM had become but a nominal shell of its original self; it had ceased to function as the quasi-fixed exchange rate system which it was designed to be.

Franc Fort Forever?

Nevertheless, Mr Balladur remained committed to the *franc fort*. The effective collapse of the ERM did not seem to make any difference. At the first cabinet meeting to be held after the adoption of the wider band, the Prime Minister made a point of stressing that nothing had happened to detract from the need for France to maintain monetary discipline and currency stability. He also chose to concentrate on fiscal injection and structural reforms aimed at job creation to stimulate the domestic economy, and refrained from resorting to further interest rate cuts.

One element of the fiscal stimulus package was a 19 billion franc income tax cut introduced into the 1994 budget. Through a revision of tax brackets, the measure was designed to be of maximum benefit to the middle classes on whose support the Balladur administration was particularly dependent. Also included were tax reforms designed to channel personal savings into housing and consumption spending.

Meanwhile, Government bonds had been issued in July 1993 in order to secure funding for additional stimulative measures. The so-called Balladur bonds turned out to be very popular, managing to raise 110 billion francs rather than the 40 billion francs originally planned. The additional resources were earmarked for such measures as spending on infrastructure investments, subsidised lending to local authorities, maintenance and repair of educational facilities, and up-front VAT rebates to businesses. It was intended that proceeds from the planned privatisation of state monopolies would pay for the redemption of the bonds.

Taken by itself, the package of stimulative measures looked impressive enough. But this was only half the story. Mr Balladur had another matter to consider: according to the convergence criteria of the Maastricht Treaty, he had to ensure that the budget deficit of the general Government sector was brought down to per cent of GDP or less by 1996. Otherwise, France would not be considered eligible to proceed to the third and final stage of monetary union, when a single currency would be introduced. France, of all EU member states, could not allow itself to fall behind schedule in the progress towards monetary union. The 3 per cent target had to be met, on time, at all costs.

To this end, the French medium-term fiscal programme envisaged the ratio falling from 4.1 per cent in 1994 to 3.6 per cent in 1995 and ultimately as low as 2.5 per cent in 1997. For 1994, planned expenditure growth was held down to a minimal 1.1 per cent. With inflation projected at 2.2 per cent, the 1.1 per cent target actually represented a decline in spending in real terms. On the revenue side, the rate of income tax withholding at source was raised from 1.1 per cent to 2.3 per cent in July 1993, and levies on petroleum and alcohol were also increased. All these measures would detract from the effect of the stimulus package; the Government was taking away with one hand what it had given with the other.

The austerity continued to dominate. The 1995 budget rejected income tax cuts and imposed an effective freeze on overall public spending. A politically brave move, it had to be said, with the Presidential election of May 1995 beginning to loom so colossally large and so close on the horizon.

Nevertheless it cannot be denied that the preoccupation with the convergence criteria limits the ability of policy to stimulate economic growth. Caught between the Scylla of *franc fort* and the Charybdis of fiscal spartanism, the French economy sails in harsh waters. It is also a hopelessly self-contradictory situation, since robust economic performance is clearly the answer that meets the requirements of both *franc fort* and the 3 per cent deficit threshold, and yet it is precisely those two elements of policy that are inhibiting the pursuit of faster economic growth.

There is nothing wrong with rigorous monetary and fiscal discipline. In the absence of an external framework such as the gold standard to guard against expansionary licence, self-imposed austerity serves an economy in good stead. That, however, is provided the discipline has been imposed for the right reasons. This has not been the case for France. Neither the staunch adherence to *franc fort* or its eagerness to meet the Maastricht Treaty's fiscal convergence criteria have been motivated by purely economic concerns. Political objectives have always been the driving force; the objectives of keeping the Franco-German tie firmly intact, and of making monetary union happen at the earliest possible opportunity. Both are seen as imperative if Germany is to be forever safely contained within the framework of the European Union, never to be tempted into seeking a new destiny beyond the confines of that relationship. Those concerns tend to render French policy oblivious to the immediate needs and plights of the economy.

Franc fort is not so much a policy in pursuit of domestic monetary stability as one of ensuring that the D-Mark is safely anchored within the ERM. It is a device for tying Germany down to a path leading to monetary union, at the centre of which the D-Mark and the French franc co-exist as key currencies. This is the goal that makes the French obsession with *franc fort* such an all consuming one.

If price stability had been the principle objective of *franc fort*, there would have been no need for the French economy to suffer so much for so long. Taking the cue from German nominal rates had brought about that situation. French inflation had fallen below 2 per cent, at a time when German prices were still increasing by more than 3 per cent. There was no sound economic reason why French nominal interest rates should stay above those of Germany in the circumstances. Yet this was what happened, and the consequences were suffered by French companies in the form of punishingly high real interest rates. Similarly, given the depth of the unemployment problem, fiscal policy could have been allowed greater freedom to stimulate the economy. The convergence criteria did not allow this to happen.

Whatever the motives, it is always dangerous to apply economic tools for the sake of political objectives. While the return to positive economic growth and the easing of German monetary policy have allowed the problem to recede for the time being, nothing has actually changed. Once German interest rates begin to rise, as they must do, the essentially self-destructive nature of French economic management is bound to resurface.

Indeed, there may come a time when the *franc fort* policy itself begins to endanger the franc's position *vis-à-vis* the D-Mark. If, for the sake of *franc fort*, France is forced into a premature return to rising . interest rates; this could result in an actual weakening of the franc against the D-Mark, since the higher interest rates will be seen as nipping economic recovery in the bud. Far from winning the markets' confidence, rigid adherence to the *franc fort* would then become the very cause of a withdrawal of funds from franc denominated assets. Thus, soldiering on with the *franc fort* could turn into a, literally, self-defeating exercise. Investors will not feel inclined to place their bets on an economy engaged in suicidal masochism.

The marriage of convenience between France and Germany is becoming an increasingly burdensome one to maintain for both sides. Economic reality is not a thing that is easily suppressed by political necessity. At some point, France will be forced to choose between the politics of *franc fort* and the economics of full employment, as will Germany between the economics of unification and the politics of the Bonn-Paris axis.

[1] *The Independent.* 4 March 1993

[2] *ibid.*

[3] *The Times.* 3 September 1993

[4] *The Financial Times.* 4 May 1993

[5] *The Financial Times.* 26 June 1993

2

Europe's Business: Business or Politics?

"The business of the Community is not business but politics,"[1] said Walter Hallstein, the first President of the EC Commission. How has this line of thought affected Europe's approach towards closer union? How have the politics and the economics of integration combined and conflicted in that process? Political will has indeed been the crucial factor in keeping the vision of a united Europe alive over the years, in keeping the torch of closer integration alight in spite of the many difficulties encountered. Yet more often than not, when it comes to actual progress, it seems to have been the prospect of tangible economic gain which provided the predominant drive forward.

2-1 No Economic Gain, No Way Forward

Jacques Delors' Annus Horribilis

Addressing the European Parliament on 10 February 1993, Jacques Delors warned the assembly that the very ideal of an integrated Europe was now at risk. Pointing to the tendency of member states to want to "renationalise" economic policy management, he went on to say that the temptation for states each to go their own way should be firmly resisted. He would surely have preferred to sound a little more optimistic on that occasion, when he was presenting his action plan for the year to the Parliament; all the more so, given that this was the year which marked the launching of the European single market.

In the event, the subsequent plights suffered by his European Construction turned out to be even greater than Mr Delors had envisaged at the start of that year. Following an unexpectedly tortuous and bruising ratification process, the Maastricht Treaty finally came into effect in November 1993 and the European Community was upgraded to the status of European Union. But in the meantime the ERM had all but ceased to function: monetary union had been deprived of the launch pad from which it was to have taken off. The single market did not bring the kind of immediate explosion in growth momentum which was promised. Enthusiasm for continuing initiative toward closer integration seemed to be receding visibly among European citizens.

Mr Delors, more than anyone, seemed acutely aware of the crisis of confidence, threatening the ideals of European unity. In October 1993, as the Maastricht Treaty was about to come into force, he was heard making the observation that in his eyes Europe appeared to be drifting towards a free trade area of a kind promoted by Great Britain. This was unacceptable to him, and surely likewise he thought, for the founding fathers of the integration process who had authored the Treaties of Rome. He went as far as to say that if nothing were done, the Community could actually drift towards disintegration over the coming fifteen years.

No doubt there was an element of calculated scaremongering involved, designed to revive some of the weakened centralising force among member states. All the same, the extent of the anxiety he displayed was noteworthy: within the space of less than a year, his concerns had deepened from merely worrying about ideals being at stake to contemplating the actual disintegration of the union he had worked so hard to forge.

The Early Years: The Marshall Plan and the ECSC

The Treaties of Rome came into effect in 1958. Throughout the very nearly forty years of development since then, there have been many achievements and many upheavals in the path towards closer integration. The concerns of Mr Delors need to be considered within the context of that historical progress.

In June 1947, Europe was presented with the Marshall Plan, designed to assist its post-war reconstruction. April 1948 saw the setting up of the OEEC (Organisation for European Economic Co-operation) as a body to enforce the Marshall plan and to see to the distribution of funds provided under the plan; the reconstruction of Europe was underway. In the same year, Belgium, the Netherlands and the Grand Duchy of Luxembourg came together to form the Benelux customs union.

Then came the formation of the ECSC (European Coal and Steel Community) which placed the two staple industries of post-war Europe under the common control of participating member states: the Benelux three, France, Germany and Italy. The control mechanism was to be overseen by a supranational High Authority. Member states progressively did away with import controls and lowered tariffs mutually. So began the long walk towards the goal of an integrated Europe with a single common currency. It had all begun with the idea that shared responsibility and a large market free of barriers would be beneficial to the nurturing of industries basic to economic expansion.

The other important concern behind the creation of the ECSC was that nations should be prevented from succumbing to the temptation of rearmament. In the words of the French Foreign Minister and founder of the ECSC, Robert Schuman: "The solidarity in production thus established will make it plain that any war between France and Germany becomes not merely unthinkable, but materially impossible . . . this proposal will build the first concrete foundation of a European federation which is indispensable to the preservation of peace."[2]

The ECSC contributed much to the rebuilding of the two industries in question. By 1957, raw steel production had grown to precisely twice the levels of 1950 in Germany. Over the same period, French and Italian steel production expanded by 1.63 and 2.87 times respectively. Even more striking was the growth in intra-regional trade. Between 1952 and 1957, West German steel exports to the non-ECSC area rose by 132 per cent, but exports to ECSC members soared by a staggering 396 per cent. The contrast was even more striking for France, whose extra-regional exports only managed a 24 per cent growth over the same period, while exports to the ECSC rose by 223 per cent. Market integration was proving highly effective for industrial capacity rebuilding in immediate post-war Europe.

Meanwhile, overall economic reconstruction under the Marshall Plan was nearing completion, but coming up against constraints at the same time. It was becoming clear that the limited size of domestic markets was preventing nations from making the most of the production capacity that they had been able to built up under Marshall Plan assistance. They needed larger markets if economies of scale were to be enjoyed to the full.

Since trade liberalisation did feature as an aspect of OEEC activity, it was to be hoped that growth in mutual exports would provide some of the much needed additional demand. That being said, the trade liberalisation that took place at the OEEC level was of a considerably limited nature compared to the measures taken by ECSC member states. By and large, OEEC-based trade liberalisation was confined to ensuring compliance with the GATT agreements, whereby signatory nations had pledged to do away with such things as quantitative restrictions on imports and exchange controls. Domestic markets were still separated from each other by considerably high tariff barriers. Increasingly, nations were beginning to feel that those barriers had to go if Europe was to secure further economic progress. The indisputable success of the ECSC only served to enhance the awareness of the need for a wider market, unhindered by tariff barriers.

It was against this backdrop that talks began in earnest in 1955 with the aim of creating a European common market embracing all branches of industry. Discussions were launched at the foreign ministerial meeting of the ECSC, held that year in Messina, Sicily. The Messina conference authorised the setting up of a committee to be headed by Belgian Foreign Minister, Paul Henri Spaak, to flesh out ideas for more wide-ranging economic integration among the ECSC member states. Based on the committee's recommendations, which were contained in the Spaak Report of May 1956, the ECSC's members became signatories to the two Treaties of Rome in March 1957. Thus the EEC (European Economic Community) and the EURATOM (European Atomic Energy Community) were established. The treaties came into force as of January 1958. With this, Europe's immediate post-war history under the protective shadow of the United States effectively drew to a close. It was no coincidence that full convertibility was restored to European currencies in December of that same year. The birth of the EEC was a symbol of the rebuilding of Europe as an independent economic entity. It was also the starting point of the long march towards the Maastricht Treaty.

The Customs Union and Beyond

The Community's initial aim was to form a customs union, that is, to do away with internal tariff barriers and to introduce a common external tariff against the world outside. The EEC Treaty refers to any further integration going beyond the customs union in only very general terms. First and foremost, what was sought was the growth-enhancing effect of a common market free of internal obstacles to trade. And insofar as this objective was concerned, everything went remarkably smoothly.

It was envisaged that the customs union would come into effect in gradual steps over a period of twelve to fifteen years. What actually occurred was that the common external tariff had been adopted by as early as July 1967, to be followed by the abolition of internal tariffs a year later. Meanwhile, a separate common agricultural policy had also been put in place, the consequences of which continue to bear heavily down on Europe even to this day.

Having successfully established the customs union ahead of schedule, the member states gathered in the Hague in December 1969 to discuss the next step forward. They decided that this step was to be in the direction of full economic and monetary union. As a matter of procedure, it may have been the more realistic choice to concentrate on taking market integration one step further, by bringing down non-tariff barriers to trade and going about establishing the free movement of capital and labour as well as tradable goods within the Community. But the more ambitious goal of a common currency and centralised economic policy management was chosen, in the belief that the internal market could only function fully under such conditions.

Pierre Werner, Prime Minister of Luxembourg, was appointed to head a working group entrusted with the task of drawing up a plan for economic and monetary union. The outcome of the group's deliberations was presented to the member states as the Werner report, in October 1970. This envisaged full economic and monetary integration being realised over a period of ten years starting in 1971. This marks the debut appearance of the term EMU in the saga of European integration. While there is no explicit reference to a single currency, the Werner report does specify the irrevocable fixing of exchange rates as an ultimate objective of the integration process. Monetary policy would be placed in the hands of a single centralised authority. It was also stipulated that the size of national budgets should fall within certain given limits. The complete freedom of movement for goods, capital and labour was seen as a prerequisite for all the rest. Thus, by as early as the first years of the 1970s, economic and monetary union transcending national boundaries had come to be a specific goal of the European integration process.

The 1970s: A Decade of Stagnation

That, however, turned out to be very much a false start, for in retrospect the 1970s was a decade of deep gloom and disillusionment for European integration. The dollar crisis of 1971 seemingly destroyed all hopes of a cosy currency union among the Community members. They could have taken the opportunity to promote the cause of a non-dollar regional exchange rate arrangement, whereby stable currency relationships could be ensured. Yet the sudden termination of the dollar's gold convertibility was far too traumatic an event for such ideas to be considered objectively. The Community's member states were all frantic to defend their own respective currencies against the turmoil, and any semblance of co-ordinated action quickly became submerged in the general chaos.

The only development that could be regarded as a move of sorts towards monetary union was the adoption of "the snake," a system of joint floating against the dollar. This commenced in March 1972, but did not last long. As one nation after another dropped out of the system, what it ultimately amounted to was an effective D-Mark currency area, consisting of West Germany itself, the Benelux three and Denmark. Ironically, they were to be joined later by three non-EC states, Austria, Norway and Sweden which became associate members.

The oil shock followed in the wake of the dollar crisis and world-wide hyper-inflation ensued, which led on to global recession. European integration came to a virtual standstill amid the turmoil and the only development worth noting during this period was the enlargement that brought the United Kingdom, Ireland and Denmark into the Community. Far from aiming at closer integration, member states began increasingly to resort to restrictive trade measures, claiming that their declining industries and depressed regions would otherwise perish in the harsh world-wide economic environment. The only way to contain such protectionist pressures was to mount Community-wide rescue operations for the industries and regions concerned. As a result, rather than being the engine of dynamic economic growth that it aspired to, the Community was compelled to act as more of a device for income redistribution over this period.

It was only towards the very end of the 1970s that the integration process began to regain some momentum. In October 1977, Roy Jenkins, the then President of the EC Commission, urged member states to renew their efforts to meet the goal of full economic and monetary union. The call was warmly received by the West German Prime Minister, Helmut Schmidt, and the French President, Valéry Giscard d'Estaing: the two most influential politicians in Europe at the time. With their joint support, things were off to a good start, and led to the creation of the EMS, which opened for business in March 1979. The decision of those two powerful men to promote monetary union was very much a reaction to the United States' persistent neglect of a weak dollar. They felt the need to insulate Europe from the harmful effects of the United States' cheap dollar policy. The aborted attempt to build a regional currency bloc in Europe was about to be resumed.

A New Lease of Life

The story of the 1980s is a familiar one. In January 1985, Jacques Delors, now at the start of his second term as President of the EC Commission, announced to the European Parliament that he would set as his aim the completion of a single European market by 1992 year-end. The Commission produced its White Paper on the subject, *Completing the Internal Market* in June that year, identifying the barriers to trade which were yet to be eliminated, and putting forward ideas on how further trade liberalisation within the Community might proceed. The white paper formed the basis for the Single European Act, to which Community member states became signatories in February 1986, pledging to establish the single market in time for Mr Delors' target of year-end 1992.

The EMU was also given a new lease of life by the "Delors Plan" of April 1989, which mapped out the, by now, well-known three-step approach towards the introduction of a single currency within the Community. At the European Council meeting of June 1989, held in Madrid, it was decided that the Community would enter phase one of the Delors Plan as of July 1990. Six months later, at the Strasbourg summit, member states agreed to start intergovernmental talks on the amendments to the Treaty of Rome which would become necessary in order to proceed to the second and third phases of the Delors programme. In April 1990, Helmut Kohl and President Mitterrand of France made a joint appeal to the rest of the Community members, urging them to open a second intergovernmental conference on political union which would proceed alongside the talks on EMU. The two sets of talks began in December that year. A year later member states reached agreement on the Maastricht Treaty.

The rapid progress achieved in those years of the latter 1980s and early 1990s was truly dazzling. While much of this achievement was clearly attributable to the presence of Jacques Delors, the great campaigner for Europe, the overwhelmingly important factor which accelerated the pace of progress was German reunification. The political concern, that unified Germany should be kept safely within the confines of the European Community, was spurring the member states towards greater and faster integration. It was a predominantly French concern, but one that was shared by the majority of the other members states. With the exception of Britain, all felt that closer and faster union was the appropriate response to the abrupt emergence of a unified Germany. Germany itself was acutely aware of the need to pledge its commitment to European unity and, moreover, to demonstrate the strength of Bonn-Paris solidarity.

Thus, German unification appeared to breathe yet more new life into the integration process. And subsequent achievements have, indeed, been quite remarkable. Agreement on the Maastricht Treaty was reached within the space of just over a year following the birth of unified Germany, and the European Union has since become a fact of life rather than a distant goal. It looked as though the political will to keep unified Germany on board had worked wonders. And yet by 1993, Mr Delors had become so disillusioned by developments that he had to wonder if Europe might not be degenerating into a mere free trade area.

The People Revolt

A look at developments following the agreement on the Maastricht Treaty reveals the reasons for Mr Delors' concerns. The first sign of trouble was the Danish refusal to ratify the Maastricht Treaty. On 2 June 1992, Denmark held a referendum on the issue, and the people voted against ratification, albeit by a thin majority. On the heels of that vote came Denmark's surprise victory over Germany in the European football championship finals held at Göteborg, Sweden. This prompted the remark: "If you can't join them, beat them"[3] from the eminently quotable Danish Foreign Minister, Uffe Ellemann-Jensen. He went mischievously on to note that "it shows small states can win, and Europe needs small states."[4] The Danish 'no' vote was the small state's revolt against the larger states' orchestrated aims of European integration. In true *sumo* fashion, the little man had thrown the larger men off balance.

The Danish rejection of Maastricht sent shock waves across the Community, and served to uncover anti-Maastricht feelings elsewhere, which may, otherwise, have remained hidden. In an attempt to prevent the dissent from spreading further, President Mitterrand promptly announced that France, too, would hold a referendum on Maastricht, even though there were no constitutional requirements for one to take place: the French people would demonstrate how solidly behind the Maastricht Treaty they were by endorsing its ratification with an overwhelming majority. Voting was set for 21 September.

But before the French people had even had the chance to go to the polls, an event occurred which effectively rendered their vote meaningless. With just four days to go to polling day, Black Wednesday descended on the ERM; repeated speculative assaults on the weaker EMS currencies culminated in sterling and the lira's departure from the ERM, and the Spanish peseta's enforced devaluation by 5 per cent. With such turmoil in progress, the French referendum was doomed to oblivion. Nor was the outcome the resounding endorsement that President Mitterrand had hoped for. The 'yes' camp only managed to come out on top with an almost non-existent 0.02 per cent majority.

The Danish problem became a key issue at the December 1992 European summit held in Edinburgh. A solution had to be found on the basis of which Denmark could hold a second plebiscite on Maastricht with a fair chance of securing a positive outcome this time round. In the end, Denmark was allowed to opt-out from virtually everything that it was likely to find objectionable: European citizenship, the single currency, common defence, co-operation in the fields of justice and internal security. With so much out of the way, there was not very much left of the Maastricht Treaty for the Danes to vote over.

After the turbulence experienced in 1992, 1993 seemingly got off to a good start, with the single market coming into effect at the start of the year, and a predictable 'yes' vote secured in the second Danish referendum on 18 May. Tranquillity was short-lived, however, and the summer months brought on another onslaught of currency turmoil, leading to the adoption of the ERM wider band. Meanwhile, Britain finally ratified the Maastricht Treaty after much bizarre wrangling within the Conservative Party, over which the party looked as though it might tear itself apart. But endorsement by the British could have offered little solace to the, by then, habitually depressive Jacques Delors. Maastricht or no, Britain would always go its own way.

Of far greater consequence for Mr Delors was the outcome of deliberations by the German constitutional court on the Maastricht Treaty. The ratification debate itself had already been completed by the 1992 year-end in both chambers of the German parliament, but increasingly vociferous anti-Maastricht campaigners had taken to questioning the constitutionality of the Treaty. Some twenty law-suits had been filed by them, and the Karlsruhe court chose to take up three of them. Rulings on those suits were due during October 1993.

The court judged in favour of the Maastricht Treaty in all three cases. This was the good news. However the court had qualified its endorsement by stressing the importance of national democratic controls. "If an association of democratic states takes on sovereign tasks and exercises sovereign powers," said the judges, "it is principally the peoples of the member states who must legitimate this through their national parliaments." Furthermore, "If, as is currently the case, the peoples convey democratic legitimation through national parliaments, then the principle of democracy sets limits on the expansion of the tasks and powers of the European communities. The German Bundestag must retain substantial tasks and powers."[5] It was bad enough for Mr Delors that in Germany of all places, attempts to bury the Maastricht Treaty had involved such an august institution as the constitutional court. That the Karlsruhe court had sounded this strong note of warning against the supranational concentration of power was a further blow which will surely cast long shadows on the integration process beyond Maastricht.

A Conflict of Interests

If there is one thing to be said about the thirty-six year journey from Rome to Maastricht, it is that the decade from the birth of the Treaties of Rome to the establishment of the customs union in 1968 was a time in which there were clear and strong economic grounds for pursuing closer integration. Without it, Europe would have simply been unable to generate adequate growth momentum. The creation of a common market was a matter of survival. There was little room to argue otherwise.

But what of the years thereafter? Can it be said that the economic case for further integration has remained as unambiguous as it was in the first ten years? The stagnation of the 1970s may justly be said to have had causes beyond Europe's immediate control. Yet it can also be argued that had closer integration been seen as providing the means to overcome the economic difficulties of the time, the process would have moved forward, notwithstanding the dire global environment. Mr Delors' single market initiative was greeted enthusiastically enough by the member states. But to what extent can this be regarded as a reflection of the intrinsic economic merits of the programme? Was it not that because their economies had started growing again, member states felt themselves capable of absorbing the costs involved in adjusting to the single market, even though competition would be keener? It is always easier to be adventurous when the economic outlook is rosy.

As for developments beyond 1989, it can only be said that the issue of economic merit appeared to have very little to do with them. Underlying economic forces seemed to be pulling the member states away from, rather than closer to one another. Why else did the ERM have to adopt the wider band, the Maastricht Treaty meet with such popular resistance, and Jacques Delors fear the disintegration of the European Construction? Yet the weakening of the centralising economic pull was, and indeed continues to be, resolutely ignored. The Maastricht Treaty was created in a vacuum: an incubator which carefully and deliberately sealed Europe off from the gale force winds of change blowing around it. That was the political choice. But the infant had to be let out of the incubator at some point. When it did climb out of the protective cot, what greeted it was not the convergence of political legitimacy and economic gain that had made closer integration such a golden dream in the first ten years of European integration: it was plunged into a world in which Europe was caught in a tug of war between political urgency and economic satisfaction.

2–2 Europe and the British Yardstick

Continental Europe has always tended to advocate the Walter Hallstein axiom of "politics before business" as the rationale for closer integration. The perspective is a very different one in Britain. "The business of the Community should be nothing but business" would best describe the attitude. When the British show no apparent interest in European unity, this is a sure sign that nothing much is happening on the economic front. If, on the other hand, Britain suddenly wants to have a finger in the pie, the economic gains to be had from pushing integration forward can be judged as considerable. In this sense, the invariably pragmatic if not prosaic British are providers of a convenient yardstick against which the economic pros and cons of European integration can be measured. Moreover, the extent to which the politics and the economics of European integration are either in harmony or in conflict with each other can also be assessed by

Britain's attitude towards the integration process. In January 1963, Charles de Gaulle said of Britain that: "England in fact is insular, maritime, bound by her trade, her market, her supplies, to countries that are very diverse and often very far away . . . How can England, as she lives, as she produces, as she trades, be incorporated in the Common Market?"[6] This was on the occasion when he announced his intention to veto Britain's entry into the European Community. How right he was. Yet it is precisely because of this insularity, this essential "otherness" that the British yardstick is effective.

From Splendid Isolation to Reluctant Partner

The evolution of Britain's relationship with Europe can be broken down into roughly five phases. Phase one: the period from 1951 when the ECSC was formed to 1958, the year the Treaties of Rome came into force. Phase two: the 1960s and the early 1970s, up to 1973, when Britain joined the European Community. Phase three: 1974 to 1978. Phase four: the Thatcher years of 1979 to 1990. Phase five: the period thereafter.

The British attitude towards European integration was at its coolest in the first phase. The Government of Clement Attlee responded disdainfully to the invitation to join the ECSC. Less bruised by the war, Britain did not share the sense of urgency with which the continental Europeans had to go about rebuilding their coal and steel industries. Nor was Britain as mindful as they of the need to exercise common control over the Franco-German industrial heartland that lay sprawled across their borders. What worried the British most was the idea of their major industries being placed in the hands of some supranational authority. They were also wary of being sucked into a "federalised" Europe via the ECSC mechanism. Moreover, Britain still felt that it had the lead on the continental Europeans as an industrial nation. It did not think that its industries required the kind of assistance that those on the continent needed.

Britain also kept its distance while the six members of the ECSC went on to form the EEC. Britain was by no means oblivious to the remarkable achievements of the ECSC, nor of the resulting erosion of its own economic supremacy in Europe. But on the other hand there was the British Commonwealth to think about. The existence of this alliance ruled out the possibility of Britain taking part in a customs union with the ECSC six, since this would have meant the erection of tariff barriers against the Commonwealth member states. Instead,

Britain came out with a "grand design" of its own regarding the creation of a European free trade area. This proposal, however, was dealt a dismissive cold shoulder by the ECSC members. So ended act one of the story of Anglo-European relations, with a visible rift dividing the two sides. The economic pull of the European partnership was not yet strong enough for Britain to contemplate abandoning its traditional "special relationship" with its Commonwealth partners.

But circumstances were beginning to take a clearly different turn as the curtain rose on act two of the tale. Increasingly, the special relationship was turning into a liability for Britain with little economic gain to compensate for shouldering the burden. The Commonwealth member states, for their part, were beginning to distance themselves from Britain in a search for a greater autonomy which their improving economic performance warranted. Moreover, EFTA, Britain's answer to the European Common Market, was not reaping the fruits that had been anticipated. It was time for Britain to reassess its options.

It was eventually decided that the EFTA had to be abandoned, and a serious attempt made to join the European Community. Entry negotiations began in 1961, but was aborted by Charles de Gaulle's refusal to accept "insular, maritime" Britain as a member. Another attempt was made in 1967, only to be blocked, yet again, by Charles de Gaulle's intervention. It was only in 1973, after de Gaulle's departure from office, that the Government of Edward Heath succeeded in taking Britain into the European Community; twelve years after the first approach. Yet the irony of it all was that by this time the economic merits of EC membership had become less indisputable than they had once seemed. For one thing, the customs union had progressed beyond the initial stages where the positive growth effects are at their maximum. Moreover, this was now the 1970s when, in sharp contrast to the golden 1960s, the world had become a place of great turmoil and stagnation. The EC was rapidly losing the economic glitter that had lured Britain into joining. Even the ferociously pro-European Mr Heath began to quarrel with the other member states over contributions to the EC budget and would not commit himself to a further deepening of European integration.

Phase three began turbulently with the new Labour Government, under Harold Wilson, embarking on a renegotiation of Britain's terms of entry into the Community. Budgetary issues left behind by the Heath Government were at the heart of those negotiations, and the hectoring tone of the Wilson Government's demands were not well received by the other member states. James Callaghan took over as Prime Minister following Mr Wilson's resignation, but this did not improve matters. Britain maintained its traditional links to the United States, while the ever-intimate Franco-German alliance was becoming thoroughly disillusioned with the Carter administration's handling of economic policy. Under the stewardship of Helmut Schmidt and Valéry Giscard d'Estaing, the two countries tabled a joint proposal for the establishment of the European Monetary System. Britain, while it became a member of the EMS, chose not to participate in its exchange rate mechanism, for fear of the prospective deflationary influence that a linkage with the D-Mark might exert on the domestic economy.

Mrs Thatcher and the British Budget Question

The Thatcher era constitutes phase four of the Anglo-European relationship. It is perhaps useful to observe this period from two angles. One, Mrs Thatcher's handling of the series of European summits in which she participated. And two, her attitude towards exchange rate policy and the EMS.

For the most part, the EC summit meetings during the Thatcher years revolved around the two themes of the EC budget and how to proceed with the integration process beyond the single market. The size of Britain's contribution dominated much of the long hours spent over the budgetary debate. This was an issue over which Britain had never ceased to complain since more or less day one of its entry into the Community. With impeccable timing, the climax came with the appearance of the Iron Lady on stage.

Having staunchly and persistently shunned starry-eyed idealism as a basis of European integration, and with the nation's balance sheet *vis-à-vis* the rest of Europe always at the forefront of its concerns, Britain was not about to waste a loose penny in contributions to the EC budget. Moreover, the Thatcher Government had come into office arguing forcefully for a smaller government as the cornerstone of British economic revival. Mrs Thatcher could ill afford being seen as an accomplice to the swelling EC budget, whilst preaching the virtues of self-assistance and balanced national budgets to her electorate. Furthermore, it was imperative that she should not be seen as paying more into the EC budget than she was getting out of it.

As for carrying European integration further, little needs to be said of the Thatcher Government's position. Mrs Thatcher's ultra-minimalist approach to the integration process and the determination to surrender as little national sovereignty as possible became the cause of her eventual almost total isolation within Europe. Nonetheless, because of the very extent and openness of her suspicions, a study of her reaction to whatever new proposals that came out of Brussels provides useful insight into the nature of those proposals. If Mrs Thatcher was willing to bury her anti-integration sentiment and go along with a certain project, then there were sure to be some very clear economic rewards involved. The single market is the obvious case in point. On the other hand, if she displayed her customary incorrigibility, this would be a sign that the proposal offered little in the way of economic merit, however significant its political implications might be. Indeed if the political implications were too great, this would draw out her intransigence all the more. Any move that would lead to more institutional centralisation was anathema.

Mrs Thatcher made her European Council role debut at the Strasbourg summit of June 1979. On this occasion, her performance was a suitably, if uncharacteristically, subdued one. But the following Dublin summit in November was an entirely different affair. It was at this meeting that her formidable campaign to get her "own money back" from the Community began.

Britain's complaint against the EC budget was that while it was being made to pay what it considered to be an unduly large sum into the EC coffers, it received very little in return. The complaint was certainly not without reason, since in 1979 British contribution to the EC budget had amounted to one-fifth of the total revenue, while Britain benefited almost not at all from the common agricultural policy, which took up 70 per cent of the expenditure side of the budget. Britain was in fact the largest net contributor to the EC's revenue. The only other net contributor was West Germany. Considering that at the time Britain ranked only seventh among the then nine EC members in terms of per capita GNP, there was clearly something incongruous about its position alongside the rich Germans.

This curious situation was, for the most part, a result of how contributions to the EC budget were structured. The so-called "own resources" of the EC, i.e., that part of its revenue which is automatically channelled into the Community's budget without being subjected to the discretion of national governments, is composed of: (a) the common external tariffs levied on manufactured goods imports from outside the community, (b) the import surcharge on agricultural imports based on the common agricultural policy, and (c) a fixed proportion (then 1 per cent) of member states' VAT intake. As such, the formula could not have been better designed to tap British coffers.

Because of its association with the Commonwealth nations, Britain imported considerably larger quantities of manufactured goods from outside the EC compared with the other Community members. It also tended to import more agricultural products. Moreover, Britain was experiencing something of a consumption boom at the time, because of the Government decision not to raise income taxes. This sop to the electorate had been made possible by the revenue-enhancing effect of North Sea oil. Delighted consumers increased their spending and the resulting higher level of the Government's VAT revenues led, in turn, to an automatic increase in the British contribution to the Community's own resources. Furthermore, while Britain's farming population is small, it was not a net exporter of agricultural produce. The various subsidies available under the CAP, accordingly, held little attraction for Britain. As Keynes would have put it, Britain was set to become the "milch cow" of Europe whichever way one looked at the situation.

Mrs Thatcher was not prepared to accept such a role for her country, and demanded compensation for Britain's net payments into the EC budget. Threats were made that Britain would refrain from contributing to the EC budget altogether if her requirements were not met. So single-minded was her pursuit of those claims that at one point President Mitterrand of France felt obliged to cast doubt on Britain's continued membership of the Community.

The British budget problem was eventually resolved at the Fontainebleau summit of June 1984. Instead of the series of one-off rebates that Britain had managed, with much sound and fury, to extract from the Community thus far, it was decided at Fontainebleau that from then on Britain would receive regular paybacks according to a given formula. Starting in 1985, annual compensations were to be made to cover 66 per cent of the difference between contributions made from British VAT takings into the EC budget and what Britain received from the Community. Thatcherite tenacity had delivered victory, and the almost Five-Year long war of the budget had reached a cease-fire of sorts.

Other points of contention emerged between Britain and Europe, even as the war of the budget was in progress. There was the argument over institutional reform, where Mrs Thatcher protested against the strengthening of the powers of the European Parliament, and to the introduction of more majority voting in the Council of Ministers. Her ideas were presented in the paper *Europe – The Future* at the Fontainebleau summit of June 1984. In short, its argument was that completion of the single market was all that was needed, and that anything else was uncalled for meddling.

Mrs Thatcher and the ERM

Moments of lively confrontation were also to be seen regarding the "social dimension," i.e., the issue of the advocacy of workers' rights within the Community. In September 1988, Jacques Delors took the daring step of addressing the British TUC at its annual conference, arguing that ". . . 1992 is much more than the creation of an internal market abolishing barriers to the free movement of goods, services and investment . . . ," that it was necessary ". . . to improve workers' living and working conditions and to provide better protection for their health and safety at work."[7] Mrs Thatcher's enraged rebuttal, conveyed through her speech at the College of Bruges in Belgium and in her address to the Conservative Party Conference in October of that year, was that: "We haven't worked all these years to free Britain from the paralysis of socialism only to see it creep through the back door of central control and bureaucracy in Brussels."[8] The allusion to socialism through the back door would invariably emerge thereafter, whenever the social dimension became a subject of Anglo-European debate.

Mrs Thatcher's final battle with Jacques Delors took place over monetary union. In an extraordinary session of the European Council held in Rome over 27 and 28 October 1990, the other members of the European Community agreed that they would move on to the second phase of the Delors plan in January 1994, setting up the European Monetary Institute in preparation for the establishment of the European Central Bank. Refusing to have anything to do with such a plan, Mrs Thatcher claimed that the other eleven were living in "cloud-cuckoo-land" if they thought such a development desirable. This occasion was to mark the beginning of the end of Mrs Thatcher's dominance in British politics, leading to her dramatic departure from office in November that year.

Throughout all these clashes with her counterparts on the continent, Mrs Thatcher's position was as consistent as it was unyielding. Only the single market with its immediate and tangible economic gain was acceptable; all the rest belonged in the realm of cloud-cuckoo-land. But where matters concerning the EMS and foreign exchange rate policy were concerned, her response lacked some of its consistency of purpose.

At the start of the EMS in 1979, the Government of James Callaghan had decided that Britain would join the system but would not take part in its Exchange Rate Mechanism. Mrs Thatcher chose to retain that policy under her Government. Yet from the point of view of economic merit, the more practical choice at the time would have been to join rather than to stay out of the ERM. The discipline that a quasi-fixed exchange rate system imposes on domestic economic management would have been consistent with her Government's stated economic aims of price stability and fiscal austerity. The ERM of those earlier years had not yet been thrown off balance by German reunification; it would have served Mrs Thatcher well in her purpose of rebuilding a British economy not hampered by chronic inflationary pressure and spending overruns. Such reasoning, however, appears to have been lost on the Prime Minister in her preoccupation with sovereignty and dislike of a currency regime built around the D-Mark.

The rift that opened up between Mrs Thatcher and her Chancellor of the Exchequer, Nigel Lawson, over the ERM is well known. Mr Lawson advocated entry into the ERM, and when his recommendations were rejected, chose to follow the course of "shadowing the D-Mark" which angered his Prime Minister even further. In any event, economic management would arguably have been easier, at that point in time, had Britain not chosen to stay out of the ERM. Fixed exchange rate systems are by no means intrinsically undesirable. It is only when they are pegged to a currency whose economy is losing its ability to maintain equilibrium that those systems begin to cause problems for its participants. That time had not yet arrived for the ERM, although it did come subsequently.

Thus it may be said that on this occasion, British refusal to join the ERM did not serve as a particularly good gauge of the economic merits offered by closer integration. On other hand, it could be argued that since Britain was unable to recognise the beneficial effects of the ERM at the time, and suffered the consequences in the building up of the bubble economy, it did after all act as a yardstick, of sorts, by way of negative confirmation.

From Handbagging to Social Dumping

In what appeared to be a marked softening of attitude towards Europe from the Thatcher years, her successor John Major announced that he wished to place Britain "at the heart of Europe." The remark won him favour with the German Chancellor, Helmut Kohl, who considered it a welcome change from the proud isolationist posture of his predecessor. But by the end of the Maastricht summit of December 1991, the Dutch Prime Minister, Ruud Lubbers, who as host to the meeting had the unenviable task of mediating between Mr Major and his counterparts, was saying on Dutch television: "The difference between Mrs Thatcher and Mr Major? The handbag."

Indeed, for all the subsequent criticism showered on him by his own party's Eurosceptics, Mr Major's points of reference in regard to the European Union seem just as prosaically oriented towards economic gain as those of his predecessor; possibly more so. He was heard saying, "There is only one aim at the heart of our European policy, the cold calculation of Britain's national interest."[9] He advocated the introduction of the 'hard ECU' as a parallel thirteenth European currency, seeing this as a more realistic approach to monetary union than the dash for a single currency. He opposed the strengthening of the social dimension of the European Union, on the grounds that this would lead to higher costs for businesses, declining industrial competitiveness and the increasing loss of employment opportunity throughout Europe. With such arguments to support his position, he won the renowned opt-out from the single currency provision of the Maastricht Treaty, and succeeded in effectively having the social dimension removed from the provisions of the Treaty proper. The other eleven member states were obliged to adopt a separate agreement on social policy, which stated their aim of continuing along the path laid down in the 1989 Social Charter, to which they, but not Britain, were already signatories.

The British attitude is not necessarily a commendable one. The unwillingness to accept exchange rate discipline, and the readiness to opt for lower costs rather than higher labour standards almost seem to represent a policy inclination to promote social dumping. Indeed, when Jacques Delors saw the outcome of debates over the social chapter of the Maastricht Treaty, his observation was that from then on, all inward investments into Europe would be snatched away by Britain. Should that turn out to be the case, the other member states will wish to take counter-measures. Some of them may feel compelled to suspend their loyalty to a common social policy and engage in social dumping policies of their own. Others may even chose to impose restrictions on British made imports.

The British lack of team spirit does harbour dangers of setting off such retaliatory crossfire. Yet the inability to keep this heretic on board may be a sign of inherent weakness in the economic reasoning behind the Maastricht Treaty. Prospects are bleak for the European Union if it lacks the magnetism to attract the most mercenary-minded of all its members.

[1] Shintaro Kishigami & Tomoyoshi Tanaka (Eds.), *The EC 1992 Handbook.* Tokyo. 1989

[2] Pinder, John. *European Community: The Building of a Union.* Oxford. 1991

[3] *The Financial Times.* 27 June 1992

[4] *ibid.*

[5] *The Financial Times.* 13 October 1993

[6] George, S. *An Awkward Partner: Britain in the European Community.* Oxford. 1990

[7] *ibid.*

[8] *ibid.*

[9] *Europe*, No. 5985. 22 May 1993

3

The Crumbling Cornerstones of Unity

3–1 On the Brink of Exchange-Rate Wars

On 10 September 1992, John Major was in Glasgow, attending a meeting of the Scottish CBI, where he categorically ruled out the possibility of a sterling devaluation. He referred to devaluation as an inflationary and cowardly option which would destroy the future of the British economy. He was not prepared to adopt such "quack doctors' remedies" and claimed sterling's ERM parity would be maintained at all costs. His utterances were accompanied by mounting tension in the foreign exchange markets, where nervousness had been pervasive ever since the first Danish referendum in June that year, with speculative interest gradually zooming in on sterling. Mr Major's show of determination made headline news that evening. Yet silence would have stood him in better stead, for it was on 16 September only a week after his Glasgow speech, that Britain was forced out of the ERM.

Black Wednesday

The ERM was launched in 1979 with eight members: West Germany, France, Italy, Denmark, the Benelux three, and Ireland. There have been three distinct stages in its subsequent development, the first of which was the period up to March 1983. The ECU parities of the ERM participating currencies underwent no less than seven revisions in that four-year period. This was the ERM's start-up phase, when the great disparity in economic performance, as well as policy management among member states, made it difficult to maintain stable currency relationships. Then came seven years of almost total bliss which lasted up to 1990. Disturbances that required parity realignments rarely occurred, with economic policy geared towards the common goal of stable prices. Indeed, the rates of inflation themselves tended to converge comfortably around 5 per cent. Only four realignments took place during this seven-year period. Spain entered the ERM in June 1989, and in October 1990 Britain finally became a member as well. This, however, marked the end of the ERM's second stage, its golden age. Portugal joined in April 1992, so, Greece was now the only Community member not participating in the ERM. Speculative tensions built up all too easily during this third stage of the ERM's development, invariably followed by rumours of realignment, thus the ability of the ERM to keep exchange rates stable was clearly undermined.

On 13 September 1992, amid persistent and ever more confident speculative attacks on the weaker currencies within the ERM, monetary authorities of the member states held an emergency telephone conference. They decided that to alleviate the speculative pressures, Germany would cut its interest rates (the discount rate by half a percentage point, the Lombard rate by one quarter of a percentage point), accompanied by an effective 7 per cent devaluation of the Italian lira. Much was made at the time of the Bundesbank's seeming capitulation to political pressure in its sanctioning of those rate cuts. There is little doubt that such pressures bore down heavily on the Bundesbank at the time, which may or may not have had a part to play in the outcome. What is equally certain is that there were also strong economic forces at work, arguably more difficult for the Bundesbank to resist than the political ones, which in effect made German rate cuts appear unavoidable.

Over the week leading up to those rate cuts, the Bundesbank had spent nearly 24 billion D-Marks in market intervention to support the lira. It was said to be the most massive exercise in concentrated intervention that the German central bank had mounted in twenty years. With so many D-Marks being unleashed on the market within a limited space of time, there would have been no escaping a sudden explosion of the German money supply if no counter-measures were taken. The Bundesbank had not come this far in its unflinching adherence to tight money control, notwithstanding the wrath and moaning of the other ERM members, only to pull the carpet from under its own feet at this point. Clearly, something had to be done to neutralise the effect of market intervention on the domestic money supply. This meant mopping up the excess liquidity through open market operations. Yet the problem with this solution was that it would lead to further upward pressure on already high German interest rates. Since it was those high German rates that had caused the speculative flow of capital out of Italy and into Germany in the first place, yet another shift in the upward direction would only add to the tension in foreign exchange markets already in a state of maximum frenzy. Thus it would require yet more heavy intervention in support of the lira, and so it would go on, with the Bundesbank locked in a never-ending effort to catch up with its own tail.

In order to escape from this death spiral, there was no alternative for the Bundesbank but to reduce interest rates. It was placed in the strange position of having to cut rates so that expansion of the domestic money supply could be restrained. Such things can happen when, in times of currency turmoil, market intervention is too heavily relied upon. This sequence of events was a typical lesson in how official intervention in foreign exchange markets can only work for a limited amount of time, after which it becomes a self-destructive exercise for the economies concerned.

Whatever its motives, the hope was that the Bundesbank's move would help restore the markets' confidence in policy co-ordination within the ERM, and bring an end to the immediate crisis. Disillusionment struck only two days later, on 15 September when sterling went through its ERM floor rate of 2.778 D-Marks to the pound. The Bank of England responded by raising its minimum lending rate by 2 per cent and then by a further 3 per cent in succession the next day, bringing the rate to 15 per cent. But even these drastic measures did not stop sterling from closing the day at 2.75 D-Marks to the pound. The day dawned on Wednesday, 16 September and it was finally decided that sterling would leave the ERM, accompanied by the Italian lira. There was also a devaluation of the Spanish peseta by 5 per cent, and the Bank of England's minimum lending rate was reduced to its pre-crisis level of 10 per cent. Black Wednesday had arrived.

Sterling and the lira continued to decline after their departure from the ERM, taking other weaker currencies down in their wake. The markets had set their ultimate target on the French franc, but in the meantime, the Irish punt, the Spanish peseta, and the Portuguese escudo all came under speculative fire. The peseta and the escudo were forced to devalue in November, and the punt in January 1993. The

Iberian currencies had to devalue yet again in May 1993, only to see the collapse of the ERM itself three months later.

In the eleven months between Black Wednesday and the adoption of the ERM wider band in August 1993, not only had sterling and the lira departed from the ERM, but the peseta had been devalued three times, the escudo twice, and the punt once. The contrast with the resilience of the 1983–90 period was quite startling.

All Fall Down

The peseta's devaluation in May 1993 came after a period of persistent selling pressure on the currency that had begun around March of that year. The markets were testing the extent to which the Spanish monetary authorities were prepared to raise interest rates in defence of the peseta. They had rightly perceived that this could not go on for long. Short term rates were reaching 18 per cent, with the unemployment rate about to rise above 20 per cent in consequence. There was no masking the damage the high rates were doing to the Spanish economy.

Political pressures on the Government of Felipe González were also mounting over alleged financial scandals. Even the Prime Minister's immense personal popularity looked as though it alone would no longer be enough to save his Government's skin. Audacious as ever, Mr González went on the offensive by calling for early elections, which he set for 6 June. But this did not change the markets' mood against the peseta, and the Spanish central bank had to intervene in the markets repeatedly in the currency's defence. Because these interventions took place for the most part in the forward market, official statistics did not immediately show a large drop in Spanish foreign exchange reserves. However, when the forward transactions were taken into account, it was estimated that those reserves had shrunk from some 60 billion dollars in the autumn months of 1992 to less than 20 billion dollars by the time of the May 1993 devaluation. The situation was rapidly becoming intolerable for the Spanish authorities, whose position was that they wished to have at their disposal at least 30 billion dollars' worth of foreign exchange reserves at any given time. The policy of fending off speculation through intervention was clearly reaching its limits.

Interest rates were already too high, and now intervention was running out of ammunition: the time was nigh for Mr González to throw in the towel. Reluctantly, he gave the go-ahead for the peseta's devaluation, humiliatingly close to the general election that he himself had called.

The Prime Minister's reluctance was by no means shared by the Spanish business community. A majority of its members, in fact, saw the devaluation as just what was needed for an export-led way out of the painful recession. And it was, indeed, the case that as the effect of the prior two devaluations began to filter through, Spanish exports had marched ahead, growing by an impressive 12.7 per cent between the first quarter of 1992 and the same period in 1993. Another devaluation was frankly more than welcome at this point. Moreover, industries could anticipate rate cuts, now that defending the peseta was no longer the priority policy concern. Their hopes were answered on the very day of the third devaluation with a 1.5 percentage point reduction in the market intervention rate.

The Portuguese on the other hand, felt strongly that they had become innocent casualties of the crossfire between the peseta and the speculators. The Portuguese Government had intended to use the ERM parity as a symbol of price stability, the pursuit of which would make the economy healthier and stronger. A devaluation was not at all what it had in mind. Mr Miguel Beleza, the governor of the Bank of Portugal made a point of emphasising this, saying that ". . . devaluation was neither desirable or necessary. We believe there were no fundamental reasons for the escudo to devalue. However, given the circumstances, all alternatives, including doing nothing, were worse . . . We would have preferred that none of this happened."[1]

While the Portuguese currency had been dragged down by the devaluation of a large and close next-door neighbour, the French were placed in an agonising position by an even more influential neighbour, with whom it had pledged alliance as partners in the hard currency camp. At least, this was the pledge that France had committed itself to through the *franc fort* policy: the franc must never be allowed to devalue against the D-Mark. Yet the pain that adhering to this policy entailed was becoming increasingly unsustainable. In the first instance, the *franc fort* involved keeping domestic interest rates cripplingly high in the midst of the worst unemployment situation the country had seen in post-war years. Secondly, the loss of competitiveness against the rapidly devaluing Iberian currencies, and indeed against the two defectors from the ERM, was even greater than would have been the case, had France not stuck to the *franc fort* policy. To bring the point painfully home, the franc's effective exchange rate against the other

European currencies had appreciated by as much as 8.6 per cent following Black Wednesday.

What made the situation all the more difficult to bear for France, was the fact that it depended heavily on trade with the "weakening currency group" of nations. By this time, a clear line of division was emerging. On the one side was what had begun to be referred to as the hard core group of ERM currencies, comprised of the D-Mark, the Benelux currencies, the Danish krone and the French franc, and, on the other, the devaluers' league made up of sterling, the lira, the peseta, the escudo, and the Irish punt. The more a nation exported to the latter group, the more it would suffer from their repeated devaluations. This was precisely the case for France: more or less 30 per cent of its exports went to the weakening currency group; while the ratio was 24 per cent for Germany and around 15 to 16 per cent in Britain and Italy.

The fact was that over those months the Community members states had come close to taking part in a mutually destructive series of competitive devaluations. Competitive devaluation and exchange rate wars would seem to be the essence of aggressive and predatory economic behaviour. This can certainly happen. The United States' habitual benign neglect of a weak dollar may be said to belong in this territory.

But for the European currencies in those days following Black Wednesday it was more a case of reacting to events rather than embarking on a course of systematic exchange rate dumping. Once one country had started down this particular road, others had little choice but either to follow suit or to risk being priced out of the market. A domino effect strikes, which becomes all the harder to escape the more closely linked national economies are to one another. Portugal's reluctant devaluation in response to the Spanish move was a typical example. A similar fate fell on Ireland as a result of Britain's departure from the ERM and the subsequent very large depreciation of sterling. Ireland could not have done anything else but to respond with a devaluation of its own. Had it not done so, its economy would have been devastated by the loss of competitiveness. After the devaluation, Irish authorities called for a meeting of the EC's Monetary Committee. The Irish Government made clear its frustration at having been forced into devaluation by bitterly criticising the way the ERM operated. In its view, the ERM provided no protection to small countries in the event of tensions in the foreign exchange markets. Ireland reproached the German Bundesbank for not intervening in the punt's behalf as it had done for the French franc. It also accused Britain for erratic monetary management and of effectively shutting Irish exporters out of their important British market by its aggressive cheap sterling policy.

The whole situation was clearly becoming unsustainable, and by now the adoption of the ERM wider band was an event waiting to happen. Circumstances leading up to the move have already been touched on (see section 1–3). The interest rate differential between Germany and France had narrowed to a point where it prompted French Economics Minister, Edmond Alphandéry, into his irritated call for early German rate cuts. The German Finance Minister, Theo Waigel, responded to this effrontery by withdrawing from a bilateral meeting, and from then on, storm clouds just kept on gathering.

The final blow came when the Bundesbank decided, at its last council meeting before the summer recess, to forgo a discount rate reduction. This was its decision in spite of being fully aware that France was literally praying for such cuts to take place. This brushing aside of French hopes by the Bundesbank led to the immediate collapse of the franc in the exchange markets, with the Danish krone, Belgian franc, Portuguese escudo, and Spanish peseta soon being collectively sucked into the general turmoil. In a series of emergency meetings held over 31 July and 1 August, the Finance Ministers and central bank governors of the member states came to the conclusion that the ERM would move to a wider band of 15 per cent on each side of the ECU parities, while the parities themselves would remain unchanged. Germany and the Netherlands opted to retain the original 2.25 per cent bands in a separate agreement.

Wider Band, Wiser Band?

Given the circumstances that had led to the adoption of the wider band, a more appropriate solution would have been to go ahead with an overall realignment of the ERM parities, involving a devaluation of the French franc. This, however, was clearly unacceptable to the French. To allow a devaluation to take place at this point would lead to the demise of the *franc fort* policy once and for all. The prospect of a monetary union with the Franco-German axis at its core would also be shattered. Under no circumstances could France give its consent to a franc devaluation.

The Germans, for their part, may well have wished that the ERM would collapse altogether as a result of the latest upheaval. Though that wish remained carefully unspoken, such an outcome would have freed Germany from the increasingly burdensome role as the Community's key currency nation. Germany was now a country with more than enough on its own plate, with the rebuilding of its eastern *Länder* sucking up so much of its time and energy. Life would have been a great deal easier for Germany if it no longer had to concern itself with the effect of its economic management on the other members of the ERM, and French sensitivities need not be considered with so much care. If the ERM was a straitjacket for other nations, it was also becoming a very heavy set of shackles around German ankles. Yet Chancellor Kohl, with his well-publicised conviction that German unification and European integration were two sides of the same coin, was clearly not in a position to endorse such thinking on the subject. Moreover, the Franco-German axis would collapse the moment such a lack of commitment to monetary union became apparent on the German side. A solution had, therefore, to be sought, which involved neither a franc devaluation nor anything that could lead to an, even temporary, suspension of the ERM.

Having considered a series of options ranging from the D-Mark's temporary departure from the ERM to immediate and full monetary union between Germany and France, the eventual agreement on the wider band was very much the easy way out, involving very little in the way of a fundamental solution. The general feeling was that anything was better than an overall ERM suspension. But an ERM with so much room for currency fluctuation was nothing but a caricature of the original edifice, on show for the sake of keeping up appearances.

Mr Wim Kok, the Dutch Finance Minister, called the final outcome the "second worst solution."[2] Yet adoption of the wider band was surely more a case of the worst of two worlds, since what it did was to combine the inflexibility inherent in a quasi-fixed exchange rate regime with the instability of a freely floating system. Given a 15 per cent margin of manoeuvre, the temptation to pursue a low exchange rate policy would be great. Member states had effectively been told that there would be no penalty to pay for exchange rate dumping until the 15 per cent threshold had been violated.

The situation had become totally incompatible with the basic aim of a fixed exchange rate system, in which participating countries are more or less automatically forced into pursuing policies that converge towards macroeconomic equilibrium. It was as though all logical thought had been put on hold for the sake of keeping the ERM seemingly in business. Or could the true intent actually have been to put ERM unobtrusively to rest: a euthanasia for the ERM without acknowledging the fact. One is tempted to think that this may possibly have crossed the minds of some thinkers.

With all speculative attention fixed on its every move, the French franc initially registered a near 5 per cent decline against the D-Mark after the introduction of the wider band, but subsequently managed to regain its old ERM floor. A similar path was followed by the Belgian franc, which also lost value considerably to begin with, but went on to resume its close shadowing of the D-Mark. It could almost be said that insofar as these currencies were concerned, the ERM had reverted to its original 2.25 per cent bands within a short space of time after the switch to the wider band.

The relevant question, however, is to what extent, if at all, the wider band had been instrumental in bringing about this seeming return of stability? Many would argue that the wider band was indeed the medicine that did the trick. They claim that the greater degree of allowable fluctuation made it more difficult for speculators to go on the offensive. This is true in that whereas the amount of funds needed to drive a currency down to its previous 2.25 per cent band floor was by no means prohibitively large, defeating the 15 per cent margin is quite another matter. With the 2.25 per cent band, the speculators were virtually assured victory once the selling momentum had been built up sufficiently. Challenging the 15 per cent band requires much greater resources as well as more recklessness.

Reasonable as it is, the point is, nevertheless, a technical one. It is irrelevant as to whether or not the wider-band ERM has the inherent ability to make currencies and economies converge towards equilibrium conditions. If the wider band is in fact the saviour of the ERM, it has to be shown to have internal mechanisms which work autonomously and automatically to bring about greater currency stability. Such internal stabilisers are clearly missing in the wider-band ERM. This is only to be expected, for the wider band ERM is precisely that, and nothing more. It is the ERM with wider margins of allowable fluctuation. No other features or devices to ensure greater stability have been added to the existing machinery. Moreover, there is no reason to assume that the 15 per cent barrier is unpenetrable. There is plenty of evidence to show that, even when currencies are freely floating, they can become targets of concentrated speculative attacks.

Why was it then, that relative calm was restored in the foreign exchange markets soon after the adoption of the wider band? The explanation is, in fact, quite simple. It was not the wider band ERM, but falling German interest rates which had brought about the subsequent tranquillity. The German discount rate was reduced five times in the year or so following the move to the wider band. This made it possible for the French to reduce their interest rates without jeopardising their *franc fort* policy. Much the same could be said for the other ERM members. With German rates on the decline, countries were no longer confronted with the trade-off between domestic employment creation and currency stability. Given this very substantial change in the environment, it was only to be expected that the currency market should enjoy a respite from the upheavals of the past months.

Meanwhile, nothing had changed in terms of the internal mechanics of the ERM. If it had indeed been the wider band rather than the change of direction in German interest rates that had worked the trick, France should have been able to relax its monetary policy irrespective of which way German interest rates were going. It should not have needed to wait for German rates to come down. Very much to the contrary, there was not one instance throughout this period, where French rate cuts preceded German ones. French monetary policy was still, as ever, slavishly following where the Bundesbank went. This being the case, what happens once German interest rates are once again on the rise is clearly the key issue. And there is good reason to believe that such a turning point is not too far away. Once that reversal of directions occurs in German monetary policy, the *franc fort* will again become the biting yoke that had so throttled the French economy in the months leading up to August 1993. Subsequently currency turmoil in the first months of 1995 exposed the vulnerability of the ERM even without a German rate rise.

The 1930s Revisited?

The ERM is the closest thing to a fixed exchange rate regime that exists today, although the wider band casts considerable doubt on its claim to that name. It is also the chosen vehicle by which the European Union means to arrive at monetary union. Are current conditions such that a quasi-fixed exchange rate system has a good chance of working, thereby leading to the successful switch to a single currency?

There are arguably three instances in which a system of fixed exchange rates can indeed be expected to work with reasonable success. Each may be characterised respectively by: (a) complete inflexibility, (b) complete domination, and (c) complete convergence.

The gold standard is the classical example of case (a). Here, it is the physical constraint imposed on an economy by its supply of gold reserves that guides it unerringly towards macroeconomic equilibrium and currency stability. The mechanism is as automatic as it is relentless. Case (b) is where a single nation with outstanding economic strength towers over others as the key currency nation. The Bretton Woods system at the height of its powers and the ERM itself of the 1980s can be said to belong in this category. The ERM's success story of the mid-and late-1980s clearly owed a great deal to the presence of an essentially robust German economy; its performance was the norm to which the rest of the Community member states tried to conform. As such, the German economy became the cornerstone of internal convergence and stability. Case (c) would be where complete economic convergence is achieved among the system's participants, and a single set of policies is applied to all the participants alike. In that event the system would become none other than a single currency regime. National economies of today are imperfect examples of this state of affairs; imperfect to the extent that regional diversity in economic performance exists in varying degrees at any given time, and income transfers are invariably needed to smooth out the differences. The EMU would be the other example in the event that it should be realised.

It should be clear that the ERM of today shares none of the characteristics of these three instances of a functioning fixed exchange rate system. It goes without saying that the ERM is not equipped with the automatic equilibrium-seeking mechanics inherent in the gold standard. Its days of case (b) type stability have been cut short by German reunification. Perfect convergence is certainly nowhere near being achieved at present. The convergence criteria of the Maastricht Treaty are but a poor yardstick of the depth and width of the uniformity required. Moreover, because of their simplistic rigidity, the convergence criteria pose risks of actually jeopardising rather than enhancing the macroeconomic equilibrium of the economies concerned.

Given that none of the conditions that make fixed exchange rate systems work are to be found in the ERM, it is not unreasonable to assume that the mechanism has outlived its usefulness. Indeed, current circumstances are startlingly reminiscent of those that were prevalent in the decade spanning the mid-1920s and the mid-1930s, when the world witnessed the final collapse of the international gold standard.

It was in 1931 that Britain abandoned the gold standard. Freed from the rigid austerity of the system, Britain went on to engage itself in an aggressively systematic devaluation of its currency. The United States also left the gold standard in 1933, and soon the two nations became involved in unbridled exchange rate warfare. The consequences of that warfare were more dire for the nations still adhering to the international gold standard than for the warring parties themselves. France and Germany were the major casualties of the conflict. By mid-1936, it had become increasingly apparent that, given its alarmingly depleted gold reserves, France, proud leader and staunch guardian of the gold bloc as it was, would be unable to hold out much longer. It was eventually forced to terminate the franc's link with gold in October 1936. Switzerland and the Netherlands, the remaining members of the gold bloc, immediately followed suit. This was how the international gold standard finally met its demise.

In the end, the deflationary pressures arising from the attempt to maintain the gold standard had proved just too great for France. It goes without saying that the severe loss of competitiveness resulting from the Anglo-American devaluation onslaught was an added blow. The parallel with the *franc fort* addicted France of today is quite uncanny.

Yet at a more fundamental level, the relevant comparison is between the France of those years and the Germany of today. In those final days of the international gold standard, the success of the competitive devaluation policies of Britain and the United States was contingent upon the presence of France with its adherence to the gold standard firmly intact. Without a nation willing to trade gold at a fixed price unconditionally and limitlessly, the ploy of the British and the Americans would not have been sustainable. Though not strictly exact, it is possible to draw a parallel between the position foisted on the franc in the 1930s and that which is held by the D-Mark today, to the extent that the D-Mark is a currency which does not allow itself to devalue against other European currencies. Without the presence of such a currency, it would certainly become difficult for other nations to benefit for long from competitive devaluation.

This is not to say that a Germany, less averse to a weakening D-Mark, would present a solution to the ERM's problems. Quite to the contrary, for Germany to start involving itself in the business of exchange rate dumping would be the worst development imaginable.

Without the German anchor, the ERM has little hope of retaining even what little semblance of cohesion that it still possesses.

The exchange rate wars of the 1930s eventually led to the signing of a tripartite currency agreement between Britain, France and the United States. This became the starting point for what was eventually to become the Bretton Woods system. Whether such a move towards harmony can commence in Europe among the debris left by the currency turmoils of the early 1990s remains to be seen. What is certain is that it will require more than the Maastricht time-table and even Franco-German determination to make such a development possible.

3–2 Divided We Stand: Internal Regionalism to the Fore

"Resti l'Italia a me"

The time is AD 454: *"Avrai tu l'universo, resti l'Italia a me"* (you shall take the universe, but leave Italy to me): says Ezio, a Roman general, to Attila, king of the Huns, who is on his way to conquering Europe. The famous phrase occurs in scene one of the prologue to one of Guiseppe Verdi's earlier operas, "Attila." At its premiere in March 1846 at the Teatro Fenice in Venice, the audience cheered these words in a frenzy of burgeoning nationalism, crying *"A noi! L'Italia a noi!"* not caring if the actual connotation of Ezio's utterance was that should Attila help him to take Rome, he in turn would assist Attila in conquering the rest of Italy. Such base elements of intrigue were lost on Venetians at the height of the Risorgimento, the crusade against Austrian domination and the quest for an independent Italian nationhood. In March 1848, exactly two years after the opera's premiere, Milanese citizens rose up against their Austrian oppressors in the *"cinque giornate,"* successfully driving them out of Milan, if only to be reoccupied soon afterwards.

Who Needs Maastricht?

Foreign intrusion kindled nationalistic awareness in mid-nineteenth century northern Italy, and brought out in the people the willingness to stand up against domination by external forces. As the twentieth century enters its final years, similar sentiments seem once again to be on the rise, in Italy as well as elsewhere. This time, the catalyst has been that ill-fated word, Maastricht.

The extent of anti-Maastricht sentiment caught national leaders unawares, as they set about the business of having the treaty ratified. The strongest signals of dissent manifested themselves in Denmark, where the first plebiscite on the issue, held in June 1992, returned a 'no' vote against ratification. A second referendum was held in May 1993. To secure a 'yes' vote on that occasion, lavish concessions were made to Danish demands at the December 1992 European Council meeting held in Edinburgh. At the Edinburgh summit, the Danes won opt-outs from four key areas covered by the Maastricht Treaty. They were: European citizenship, the single currency, the common defence policy, and co-operation regarding internal security. In short, virtually everything. Indeed, the then Danish Foreign Minister Uffe Ellemann-Jensen's assessment of this achievement was that: "Six months, nine days and seventeen hours after the Danish 'no' we have reached an agreement that will enable us to hold a second referendum. We have got everything we wanted".[3]

That second referendum took place on 18 May 1993 and this time the much coveted endorsement was indeed given, with 56.8 per cent of the votes in support of ratification, and 43.2 per cent against. The political leadership heaved a collective sigh of relief throughout the Community.

Yet the 43.2 per cent 'no' vote was still substantial, given that the Danes "had got everything they wanted". In Edinburgh, it had not been so much a case of the other member states bending over backwards to accommodate Danish requirements; they virtually agreed to stand on their heads, so that the view might look agreeable from the Danish line of vision. This being the case, the 'yes' camp in Denmark ought to have been able to secure a much larger proportion of the votes. Something in the range of 70 per cent to 75 per cent would not have been surprising. Yet the actual outcome was that more than 40 per cent of the populace who voted were still not prepared to give their approval to Maastricht. It should also be noted that the Government had gone so far as to announce that following ratification, it would immediately go ahead with tax reforms involving income tax reductions. So much blatant attempt had been made to appease voters, and still the 'yes' vote did not even reach 60 per cent of the total.

On the night of the second plebiscite, anti-Maastricht demonstrators took to the streets of Copenhagen, where they became involved in a confrontation with riot police. The clash was repeated the next evening, and this time, live shots were fired directly at the demonstrators. Reports claimed that it was mostly anarchist activists who were at the forefront of the demonstrations and that ordinary citizens had little to do with the affair. Nonetheless, the incident was received with great shock and dismay, not only in Denmark itself, but throughout the whole of the European Community.

These confrontations developed into the worst incidents of their kind in post-war Denmark. Street warfare lasted for five hours, with eleven young men injured on the side of the rioters and twenty-six among the police force. One citizen who had received a leg wound cried that "they shot us because we said no to Maastricht". Chilling words, even though they may have come from the lips of a calculating terrorist agitator. On the eve of the first plebiscite, a housewife taking part in a talk show had remarked bluntly that she would vote 'no' because she was not prepared to see her children being taken to war to fight for Germany. The gentle people of Denmark had been given a nasty jolt by Maastricht.

People are by nature averse to the idea of a supranational entity casting its shadow over their lives. They fear that one day such an entity may force them to send their young into unknown battlefields, that their own national Governments may be compelled to accept policies they may not otherwise pursue, and that even their own police forces may be subjected to outside meddling. Even with major opt-outs from the Maastricht Treaty such as the Danes were able to secure, to the extent that the basic blueprint of a united Europe remains, such fears are never likely to die down completely. The desire to cry out *"resti la mia patria a me"* will always come to the fore when people feel their freedoms to be at risk.

Even in Germany, the land of the D-Mark, the Maastricht Treaty was by no means received with open arms. The Bundestag did give it its approval in December 1992. But the endorsement was not unconditional. It was clearly stated that when the time came to actually consider Germany's participation in monetary union, the decision would depend, not merely on its eligibility in relation to the Maastricht convergence threshold, but on a separate vote in the Bundestag at that point. Thus, even though the Treaty itself was ratified, an effective right of veto had been retained in regard to one of its most important provisions. The Bundestag declared that in arriving at this decision, it had responded to the deep concerns held by the German people regarding the adoption of a common currency.

Even the most pro-integration minded member states do not necessarily support the idea of a literally unified Europe. Motives for supporting closer integration vary, but for the southern member states of Spain, Portugal and Greece, and also for Ireland, the reasons for their pro-Europe position are quite straight forward: they have the most to gain from being a part of the union. Their economies depend most heavily on subsidies out of the EU budget. For these poorer member states, income transfer via the EU budget is a critical element in their quest for greater growth and prosperity. Figures from 1990 show that, for Spain, receipts from the EU budget amounted to 1.46 times its contributions to EU revenues. The equivalent ratios were 2.20 for Portugal, 5.41 for Greece, and as much as 6.11 for Ireland. Given such large net benefits, being a part of the integration process has clearly been a godsend for these countries. It is not surprising to see *"resti la mia patria a me"* sentiments taking the back seat in such circumstances. But on the other hand, loyalties based on financial ties are all too easily forgotten when the money starts to run out. Political commitment is on shaky ground in the absence of economic expediency.

Subsidiarity and the Regions

Faced with an unexpected groundswell of anti-Maastricht feeling, EU Governments turned to the notion of subsidiarity in an attempt to dispel the peoples' suspicions. The concept is incorporated in Article 3b of the Maastricht Treaty: "In areas which do not fall within its exclusive competence, the Community shall take action, in accordance with the principle of subsidiarity, only if and in so far as the objectives of the proposed action cannot be sufficiently achieved by the Member States and can therefore, by reason of the scale or effects of the proposed action, be better achieved by the Community." Governments claim that so long as this provision is adhered to, there will be no fears of the member states being subjected to undue interference by Community institutions.

The term 'subsidiarity' makes its appearance at various moments in twentieth-century European history. Said to originate with Aristotle, it was used by Pope Pius XI in the encyclical *Quadragesimo Anno* in 1931, to defend the rights and freedoms of citizens against Mussolini's aggression. In post-war West Germany, the sharing out of responsibilities between the federal Government and the *Länder* was carried out according to the principle of subsidiarity. It is a notion which places maximum value on individual freedom and self-determination, and translates, in institutional terms, to the advocacy of decentralised government. In this sense, the principle can justly be regarded as the appropriate instrument of protection against excessive centralised control within the EU.

Yet if the essence of subsidiarity lies in self-determination and decentralised government, to preach it as a means of promoting European integration is more or less a contradiction in terms. Integration is a process whereby entities merge closer together and a uniform economic area is created. Subsidiarity is about individualism and the upholding of separate identities. It is difficult, at best, to see how a Europe, in which a single monetary policy presided over by a single central bank operates, could reconcile itself with the notion of a Europe governed by the principle of subsidiarity. The convergence criteria of the Maastricht Treaty speak for themselves. How can a call to converge be compatible with the idea of decentralisation and the preservation of diversity.

Notwithstanding the glaring contradictions, the fact remains that leaders needed to bring in the notion of subsidiarity to convince people and to put their minds at rest over Maastricht. This is the interesting aspect of the problem: that campaigners for greater European integration should have been obliged to resort to a concept which essentially contradicts that which they wish to achieve, in order to appease the public.

The golden dream of a united Europe loses much of its attraction when there are no readily identifiable gains to be displayed before the people. The dream can in fact all too easily change into a nightmarish image of oppression in the eyes of the people, giving rise to nationalistic forces of fragmentation and disintegration. It is these forces that have driven European leaders into seeking refuge in subsidiarity.

Nationalistic fervour is by no means unique to national states as they stand today. Awareness of nationhood, is if anything, much more fervently felt in the regions within nations. Many a country exists today, where a variety of ethnic identities and aspirations are barely contained within given territorial boundaries. The word subsidiarity rings sweet in the ears of those many different peoples co-existing inside almost every EU member state. Those peoples and regions feel that if subsidiarity be the governing principle under which the

European Union is to operate, they should be allowed to enjoy wide-ranging rights to freedom and self-government.

The official position of the Union is that subsidiarity is only applicable to the relationship between its institutions and the member states. But the regions pay little heed to such semantic escapism. They refer to the Maastricht Treaty's preamble, in which it is stated that the Union is to be a place where "decisions are taken as closely as possible to the citizen," in the belief that these words legitimate their claim to greater autonomy.

Take Belgium. Small as it is, it is a nation of two languages, two cultures and two peoples. That reality has now been officially recognised, with the move from being a kingdom to a federal state in 1993. Yet both the Flemings and the Walloons would wish to see a still greater acknowledgement of their separate identities. One complaint the Flemings have is that they are being made to subsidise Wallonia out of their own incomes. Notwithstanding the switch to a federal system, the areas of taxation and welfare still remain within the jurisdiction of the central Government. This being so, the fact remains that a more or less unilateral flow of income transfer persists between Flanders and Wallonia. Such flows run to around 100 billion Belgian francs per year, equivalent to 1 per cent of the nation's GDP.

Because of these transfers, there was a time when a "negative income paradox" had developed between the two regions: Flemings were earning more, but when the transfers had been taken into account, Walloons were actually left with the larger incomes. The situation has since been rectified due to the overall rise in wage levels in Flanders, but the transfer mechanisms are still in place, and this leaves the Flemish unhappy. On the other hand, Walloons feel they are entitled to their share of the federal takings.

Belgium's always tenuous hold on national solidarity was dealt another blow with the death of King Baudouin in July 1993. Known as *Le Roi Triste*, affection and respect for the monarch were the sentiments which held the two peoples together. Deprived of his presence, voices calling for regional autonomy are bound to grow louder.

Umberto Bossi's rapid rise to power in Italy is another case of internal regionalism at work. Though his fall from grace, at least for the moment, appears to have been just as rapid, his call for an independent Lombardy, another *Battaglia di Legnano*[4] as it were, captured people's imaginations. Northern Italy shares the grievances of

Flanders. It falls on their more affluent shoulders to support southern Italy, the *Mezzogiorno*. Southern Italy's production level amounts to only 60 per cent of the GDP of northern Italy, and it has four times the level of unemployment. The wider this gap grows, the heavier becomes the burden of transfers on the north.

There was a time when southern Italy served as both a lucrative market and a reservoir of manpower for northern Italy. But this was when the economic pie was growing persistently larger, and there was no shortage of demand for the wares being produced in northern Italy. That convenient division of labour is becoming progressively unsustainable. The distance between Lombardy and Sicily is large, in sentiment as well as geographically. Strong political will is needed to hold them together, but that political determination has to be supported by readily justifiable economic reasoning. Both are hard to come by in the present day environment.

In Spain, Catalonia accounts for one-quarter of all the industrial production. It also holds a 20 per cent share in the total GDP of the nation. The region has a strong economic base supported by its -industrious small business community. The ardent Catalan quest for independence now goes hand-in-hand with the desire to guard its economic resilience against drainage through transfer payments to the poorer regions. The combined force calling for ever greater self-rule is a formidable one.

Catalonia has a law on Linguistic Normalisation. Passed in 1983, its aim is to facilitate the widespread use of the Catalan language. Public use of the language was prohibited under Franco's rule, and the Catalans are now trying to make up for lost time. So great is their zeal that criticisms of linguistic cleansing have been heard, but the desire to establish an independent national identity knows no bounds, especially when for a time it had been suppressed by oppressors. The tenor, José Carreras, once remarked: "The more Catalan they let me be, the more Spanish I feel." The neighbouring Portuguese say that there are immediately recognisable differences between the Spaniards of the North and the Spaniards of the South. Their separate identities are crying out to be acknowledged.

In spite of their independent-mindedness, the regions within nations tend, by and large, to support European integration. This is because they see in that development prospects of greater autonomy for themselves. "Closer to Europe, further from Rome" was Umberto Bossi's slogan. Catalans have also regarded the EU as an alternative, of sorts, to complete independence from the Madrid Government. The Flemings and Walloons hope that their separate voices will be heard more directly in a Europe where national governments have less power. A similar sentiment may be detected among the Scottish people of Britain. "Closer to Europe, further from Westminster" would suit them admirably.

In short, the pro-Europe rhetoric of the regions is based on the desire for self-perpetuation. It is not because they are particularly committed to the idea of a unified Europe that they express enthusiasm for the EU as an institution. On the contrary, they will immediately turn their backs on the EU if it is seen to become just another and more meddlesome version of Rome, Madrid, or Westminster. Their invariable insistence on direct representation in Brussels is witness to the fact that the regions mean to make the most of Europe in order to lessen the hold that national governments have on their destiny. Subsidiarity and solidarity: how are these two notions to be reconciled? Only through the fear of greater enemies without, or the promise of greater prosperity within, it would seem.

The integrationists may have shot themselves in the foot by bringing in the concept of subsidiarity. Thought to be a useful tool of appeasement, it may turn out to be a hornet's nest in waiting. The following words of Luigi Farini, one of the founding fathers of the unified Italian state, sound fascinatingly relevant to today's Europe:

The political unit that we have to establish must neither be the product of an abstract conception nor an arbitrary solution. It must represent those effective natural and historical conditions that exist, and it must take into account those centres of moral suasion which exist and which, if they were suppressed, could bounce back and become dangerous. But if legitimately satisfied, they could contribute admirably to reinforce the nation. If we want to accomplish an efficacious decentralisation and give to our country the institutions that it merits, then we must in my opinion respect the natural component parts of Italy.[5]

The Price of Solidarity

The regions are significant from another perspective. This has to do with the EU's role as an income redistribution mechanism.

For many years, income redistribution within the EU was synonymous with the transfer of resources from the industrial sector to the agricultural sector. Support for agriculture was the dominant item in the EU's expenditure throughout much of its history. Financing the Common Agricultural Policy has been a major headache and the cause of many a fiery confrontation between member states ever since the CAP's inception in 1967. The problem of butter mountains and rivers of milk is well known. In spite of the major reforms that have taken place over recent years, there is little doubt that the CAP will continue to be a thorn in the EU's side well into the next century. This will be all the more so in the event that the accession of the former Communist nations of Central and Eastern Europe takes place.

Towards the mid-1970s however, a new emphasis began to be placed on the correction of geographical, as opposed to sectorial, income disparities. The adverse global economic environment of those years was one cause of this development. The other was that having established the customs union, the incremental growth-generating momentum of the Community itself was declining compared with the earlier start-up years. The economic pie had stopped growing, or at least it was no longer growing fast enough to make everyone steadily richer. The losers had to be given a helping hand, other-wise they would quickly become disillusioned and lose interest in further European integration. Income transfers were becoming a necessary sweetener to secure political acceptance for the integrationist cause.

The political significance of inter-regional income redistribution began to be felt even more strongly as the single market project took off in the mid-1980s. It was feared that with the breaking down of existing barriers to trade and the emergence of a more competitive internal market, the gap between regional winners and losers was likely to widen, and that this might cause a groundswell of anti-Europe sentiment. Measures would need to be put in place to prevent this from happening; the Community had to be equipped with the resources with which to buy cohesion. It was with this in mind that in 1988 Jacques Delors proposed a doubling of the size of the so-called Structural Funds of the Community. The proposal formed part of the "Delors package," which also included the reform of the CAP and the EC budget.

The Structural Funds are: the European Regional Development Fund (ERDF); the European Social Fund (ESF); and the Guidance Section of the European Agricultural Guidance and Guarantee Fund (EAGGF). In the early 1980s the combined resources of the three funds was apt to take up around 18 per cent of the EC budget. As a result of the Delors package, this figure had risen to 28 per cent

in 1992. It was also decided that the Structural Funds should
concentrate their assistance on five priority areas:

1. The less developed regions;
2. Areas of industrial decline;
3. The long-term unemployed;
4. Employment of the young;
5a. Structural adjustment in agriculture;
5b. Development of rural areas.

Equipped with the resources and the objectives, income redistribution
had come to hold a firmly established position within the EC's
institutional framework. This is a development that was not envisioned
in the formative years of the Community. Although the preamble to the
Treaties of Rome states that "the differences existing between the
various regions and the backwardness of the less favoured regions"
must be reduced, this was very much with the *Mezzogiorno* in mind.
After all, the original six members of the EC were nations with a
considerably high degree of economic convergence already in existence
between them. It was not thought necessary at the time to equip the
Community with elaborate mechanisms for distributive purposes.

Times have changed, however, and the Community is now a Union
of fifteen members, each with its own internal problems of diversity
and inequalities. Even among the original six, there have been
developments that call for a change of attitude towards distributive
issues, of which German reunification is the most significant.
Furthermore, the declining growth momentum makes it difficult to
dissipate "the differences existing between the various regions"
through the perpetual motion of economic expansion. There is no
longer enough of the economic pie itself to go round, and other forms
of nourishment have to be provided.

The Structural Funds form the core element of that supplementary
nourishment. A recent addition to the list is the Cohesion Fund, which
was established as an outcome of the European Council meeting of
December 1992 in Edinburgh. This is an instrument for channelling
funds into environmental protection measures and infrastructure
building in the poorer member states; poorer meaning nations with per
capita GDP levels below 90 per cent of the EU average. At present
Spain, Portugal, Greece and Ireland are eligible for assistance from
the fund. The brainchild of Spanish Prime Minister, Felipe González,
the Cohesion Fund is the clearest evidence yet that solidarity has a
price these days and that it does not come cheaply.

The further the EU tries to go down the integration path, the higher that price of solidarity is likely to rise. Depending on the specific form that monetary union might take, massive fund transfers may become necessary to smooth out income differentials. The alternative is regionally-concentrated massive unemployment, massive intra-EU migration, or both. Given the growing reluctance of the richer regions throughout the Union to provide for the poorer ones, it is questionable whether the EU will be able to muster adequate resources to prevent this happening. On the other hand, if it does fall on the EU budget to act as constant shock absorber and bailer-out for the sake of solidarity, the butter mountain that reformists worked so hard to remove will merely have been replaced by a quagmire of income subsidies for the regions.

---

[1] *The Financial Times*. 15 May 1993

[2] *The Financial Times*. 3 August 1993

[3] *The Financial Times*. 12 December 1992

[4] In 1176, the knights of the Lega Lombarda (the Lombard League) fought against and defeated the invading army of Frederick Barbarossa, German King and Holy Roman Emperor, in the battle of Legnano. The incident became the subject of Guiseppe Verdi's opera *La Battaglia di Legnano*. Premiered in 1849, the opera was Verdi's tribute to the *Risorgimento*, concealed under the veil of history to evade censorship. Legnano was one among many of the Lombard towns under Austrian occupation at the time.

[5] Robert Leonardi (Ed.). *The Regions and the European Community: The Regional Response to the Single Market in the Underdeveloped Areas*. London. 1993

4

Implosion or Explosion?

Enemies within, Enemies without

4–1 Can Deepening Bring Competitiveness?

Has closer union led to greater competitiveness for Europe? There cannot be many who can reply unequivocally in the affirmative at this point. Granted, competitiveness is not an easy thing to measure; all the more so in internationally comparable terms. Nonetheless, to the extent that the market allows only the strongest to win, and the mark of victory is high rates of economic growth that generate ample employment opportunity, the Europe of today clearly has to be consigned to the losers' camp.

Recession has, certainly, been a world-wide problem in the first years of the 1990s. Nevertheless, it cannot be denied that Europe has fared exceptionally badly. Closer union proved no protection against the worst post-war recession to hit it. Far from providing such protection, the high degree of interpenetration, resulting from the integration process, served to magnify and intensify the pan-European downturn, and to prolong the time required to climb out of its depth.

The creation of the single internal market was to have led to borderless competition within Europe which would, in turn, lead to its stronger economic performance. But what actually resulted was similarly low growth rates across Europe and the proliferation of high unemployment rates. This, after all, was to be expected in a group of economies whose individual members had only limited capacity for expansion. However many in number, the collective energy of such economies cannot be expected to reach soaring heights.

It would have been a different story altogether if a simple lack of demand had been the factor preventing strong growth performance. This was precisely the problem that confronted the European economies in the immediate post-war years. The limited size of their respective domestic markets prevented adequate rates of production growth being realised. At that time, the act of mutual market opening did much to spur economic growth. Once such an expansionary cycle is put in motion, the need for greater efficiency to meet ever higher-levels of demand stimulates the quest for better competitive performance. The greater competitiveness, thus achieved, accelerates production further, leading to more job-creation. This in turn generates higher levels of income and demand, so that a golden triangle made up of growth, competitiveness and employment is formed.

Gone are the Glory Days

That golden triangle is, however, no longer working. At the December 1993 European Council meeting in Brussels, a White Paper appropriately entitled *Growth, Competitiveness and Employment* was tabled and given approval by the summitteers. The European Commission had been instructed to put the paper together at the preceding Copenhagen summit of June 1993. It was to be the EU's definitive scenario to steer it out of the most serious loss of employment encountered in the post-war period. As such, its contents were awaited avidly.

In the words of this closely-watched report: "The measures designed to create jobs are inseparable from those aimed at reviving growth and competitiveness. The present interdependence is irreversible and makes economic growth conditional on international competitiveness: losses in competitiveness thus lead to losses in market shares and hence to job losses." Admirably put, yet the paper goes on to immediately qualify itself by pointing out that: "On the other hand, the search for competitiveness must not be to the detriment of prosperity and social progress."

These are strange words. While quite correctly maintaining that strong competitiveness is the essential factor that leads to growth and jobs, the paper then sees the need to warn against the pursuit of competitiveness in case it becomes a detriment to prosperity and social progress. Surely, growth and employment are the very sources from which spring prosperity, and indeed social progress. They are, essentially, impossible to achieve in an open market economy without competitiveness. How can it be, then, that the quest for greater competitiveness should be regarded as threatening prosperity and social progress?

In fact, this apparent self-contradiction is the very reason why the issue of competitiveness is such a contentious one for Europe. The golden triangle has ceased to function. Or, more precisely, there is now a fourth element which cannot be sufficiently factored into the tripartite relationship. This is the element of social protection.

The prosperity, of which the White Paper speaks, has to be one in which all members of society are ensured a certain minimum level of livelihood, irrespective of their individual abilities. The social progress aspired to is one through which an ever more equitable distribution is realised. During the earlier stages of economic development, the very act of winning the game, of achieving higher rates of growth and job creation brings about the desired welfare and distribution effects. But the time will inevitably come when the cost of providing those benefits begins to stand in the way of the pursuit of competitiveness, inhibits an economy's ability to grow, and leads to the loss of employment opportunity. EU member states are being confronted with this ultimate inconsistency between social equity and economic performance.

The costs involved in maintaining the welfare state are only too well-known. These include well-developed social security systems, shorter working hours, high minimum wage levels, intransigent unions, their widespread involvement in corporate management, inflexible hire-and-fire regulations and investments needed to improve working conditions. These are just some of the issues frequently discussed. All of these factors combine to raise the cost burden on companies and inhibit their ability to offer new jobs.

While economies are growing rapidly, these costs, heavy as they are, will be absorbed in the overall dynamics of expansion. The trouble starts when the pie stops getting larger at an adequate speed. Turn-of-the-century Europe is confronted with a stark choice: does it want more equity of distribution, or does it need competitiveness and jobs?

In this respect it is an error in perception to approach the problem from the perspective of "Growth, Competitiveness, and Employment" as the White Paper suggests. "Competitiveness and Welfare" or even more bluntly, "Competition or Equity" would have been the more relevant manner in which to present the problem. Expansion vs. distribution; growth vs. welfare: is Europe capable of restoring nonconflicting relationships between these aspects of socio-economic life? This is the question that needs to be addressed today.

Whither Competition?

Such truisms cannot have escaped the shrewd minds of the White Paper's authors. Yet their reluctance to tackle the problem is all too apparent. They display an unwillingness to discuss competition, as distinct from competitiveness. The paper states that ". . . the reduction in wage costs cannot be the only response to competition from low-wage countries as this might engender a sharp decline in living standards and pose a threat to the structure of European society." What then, is the solution? The answer given is that "A strategy to improve competitiveness must be based on intangible aspects: it means above all investing in human capital and more effectively incorporating the various factors of competitiveness . . . community industry could then concentrate on those areas where it possesses competitive advantages, i.e. high-value added products and services, as this would result in jobs being created mainly in highly specialised areas in sectors exposed to international competition." In short, what the White Paper advocates is the upgrading of Europe's industrial structure, so that a harmonious division of labour can be realised internationally.

There is nothing wrong with this reasoning as such. All the same, the process of competition and selection of the fittest will still be needed in order to arrive at such a relationship. Otherwise, the EU will have to reshape itself into a rigid command economy, so that resource allocation can be conducted according to a predetermined blueprint as well as timetable, in almost New Deal-like, or immediate post-war Japan-like fashion. As ludicrous as this may sound as an option, one wonders what else can be possible in the absence of competition. The White Paper remains silent on the issue. The silence can only be intentional and it is also the single most significant and serious error in judgement shown in the paper. It goes without saying that the question of how to make welfare and growth mutually compatible is not a uniquely European issue. Nonetheless, it has to be asked if Europe has not magnified the problem for itself and made it more complex by aversion and in its pursuit of convergence and uniformity.

The issue of worker welfare began to secure its position as an aspect of the European integration process in the 1980s. It was perceived at the time that something was needed to curry favour with the working people, if the deepening of integration was to regain momentum after the stagnation of the 1970s. Once again, it was the tireless Jacques Delors who led the campaign. He maintained that the integration process should not be allowed to concentrate on creating a "Europe for businessmen", but should aim at a construction that wins the support of all members of society. Only in so doing, he believed, could a truly united Europe be created.

His advocacy of the "social dimension" led to "The Community Charter of the Fundamental Rights of Workers," more commonly known as the Social Charter, which was adopted at the Strasbourg summit of December 1989. Its aim was to improve the protection of workers' rights throughout Europe, and to promote labour-management dialogue. The whole concept, which subsequently became enshrined in the social chapter of the Maastricht Treaty, bases itself on the continental European idea of the social contract, abhorred by Mrs Thatcher as "socialism through the back door."

While Mrs Thatcher's fears may have been unwarranted, it has to be said that the attempt to equalise working conditions across Europe on the basis of the social contract will tend to make Europe's internal market a less competitive place. However much the single market is enforced in terms of goods and services transactions, to the extent that the labour market is governed by stiff regulation and over-protective work practices, competition has little room to manifest its benefits. The longer-term implications of spreading rigidly monolithic labour practices throughout Europe should not be underestimated.

Time for a Bit of Jungle Warfare

The very issue of employment became the subject of a special G7 summit meeting convened in Detroit, USA, in March 1994. On that occasion, it became apparent that, while Europe was able to supply a limited number of relatively high-paying jobs, the United States could generate employment on a larger scale, albeit at lower wage levels. The more flexible work practices and the higher mobility of the labour force in the United States had produced this result.

This, of course, is another way of saying that the American people have had to make sacrifices in wage terms in order to secure a place among the employed. They are the victims of a self-impoverishing pattern of growth, which in itself is nothing that the United States can take pride in. No doubt it was the desire to avoid precisely this type of situation that had silenced the authors of the *Growth, Competitiveness and Employment* White Paper on the subject of competition. Be that as it may, it remains that in a society where competition does not function adequately, people are liable to price themselves out of the market before they have even had the chance to show what they can do.

Europeans lament their loss of competitiveness *vis-à-vis* the world outside, and of falling behind the rest of the world in economic performance. They fret over their inability to create jobs in the way that the United States is able to, and that they have been left far behind by the fast-growing Asian economies. All this is true, and the problems do need to be addressed. Yet the root of the problem would seem to lie within the Union itself. What needs to be done is to re-create a more competitive market structure in Europe. To the extent that Europe remains a place where vested interests are guarded jealously and there is no healthy competition, deepening integration stands little chance of leading to greater competitiveness.

The White Paper remains steadfastly mute on this point. There are in-depth discussions of pro-employment reforms such as better education and training, general deregulation of the labour market, worksharing and the curtailment of non-wage production costs. Yet because of the failure to address the most fundamental issue of how a more competitive market may be revived, the arguments presented cannot go beyond the infinitely complex, if not tedious, technicalities of how the individual reforms may be implemented. The White Paper is, in fact, hamstrung by its own insistence that: "The Community must not call into question the basic principles of its hard-won levels of social protection . . ." Its conviction is that ". . . they underlie the cohesion and attractiveness of European society." Yet a society which is solely concerned with equitable distribution and blind to all else cannot be expected to generate meaningful growth momentum.

One wonders what has become of the idea that Europe should create a internal market in which vigorous competition would lead to stronger growth. This was, supposedly, the motivation behind the single market initiative, but the EU's political leadership appear to have all but banished such thoughts from their minds. In an interview with *The Financial Times*, French Prime Minister Edouard Balladur soliloquised: "Can we [West Europeans] take it for granted that we will remain sufficient leaders in a sufficient number of sectors to survive in the face of countries with populations infinitely larger than ours and with levels of social protection infinitely smaller? I say we should leave this to the market, but only up to a certain point. What is the market? It is the law of the jungle, the law of nature. And what is civilisation? It is the struggle against nature."[1]

Europe's struggle against nature created the welfare state and the social contract. That is no mean achievement. Yet there comes a time when too much civilisation is detrimental to the health of an economy. The world outside is truly becoming a jungle of awesome vitality, where the young tigers and dragons of Asia proudly roam. How can Europe hope to survive in their midst, if it has forgotten the very rules and tricks of the survival game. If in its abhorrence of jungle warfare, Europe chooses not to play the game, no amount of technically intricate discourse over competitiveness is likely to reap much substantive fruit. Europe's alternative in that event can only be to erect a protective and prohibitive wall around itself.

Without wishing to sound like a Thatcherite spokesperson, the reluctance to address the subject of competition and the mental attitude this implies is a matter of serious concern. Europe must not allow itself to become a mutual-aid society of the weak.

4–2 Widening without Disintegration: A Feasible Option?

As of January 1995, the European Union became a community of fifteen states. The newcomers are Austria, Sweden and Finland. They were to be joined by Norway, which had concluded entry negotiations alongside the other three nations in March 1994. But in a referendum, the Norwegian people refused to give their endorsement to the accession agreement negotiated by their Government. They had repeated their performance of 1972, when they had likewise said 'no' to joining the European Community. Austria's alpine neighbour, Switzerland, has also chosen to stay out. Indeed, the independent-minded Swiss have even said 'no' to the much looser ties sought under the European Economic Area (EEA) relationship between the EFTA and the EU, which was inaugurated in January 1994.

The Way North

Enlargement talks with the EFTA members have taken many a twist and turn since they first began. They began in the mid-1980s with the EFTA side keenly seeking entry into the EC. This was quite a change in the wind, since it was in the quest of a viable alternative to the European Community that EFTA had been created in 1960. Twenty-odd years on, however, EFTA had become a very different beast from that with which Britain once sought to compete with the EEC.

The Nordic member states of the EFTA and their Alpine partners are geographically far apart. There is, also, little to link them together in economic terms. Other than the fact that they are all relatively small nations with well-developed welfare systems, they have nothing much in common. The EFTA of the 1980s, (comprising of Norway, Sweden, Finland, Iceland, Switzerland, Austria and Liechtenstein) was beginning to look increasingly redundant. There was now a conspicuous lack of rationale as to why there should be such an integrated economic area. Intra-regional trade was by no means of overwhelming importance. On average, the ratio of such transactions to total trade hovered around the 15 per cent mark. On the other hand, trade with the EC had come to take up more than half the EFTA's overall trade with the rest of the world.

Meanwhile, Jacques Delors had launched his single market initiative. Given the high rate of dependence on trade with the EC, this was a move from which the EFTA nations simply could not afford to be excluded. Moreover, there was a noticeable recovery of growth momentum across the EC which made the idea of a borderless EC-wide market appear even more attractive. Quick action was required to establish access.

The EC side's response to EFTA overtures was at best ambiguous. It was reluctant to extend membership to newcomers at a time when the club was about to upgrade its services to existing members. Indeed, the EEA was seen very much as a device with which to keep the EFTA nations at bay, to deflect them from applying directly for full EC membership. The EFTA nations, for their part, had quite different ideas, and saw the EEA as a convenient gateway into the heart of the EC. In the end, however, they did not bother to wait until the EEA was actually launched before they began their preliminary approach towards entry negotiations with the EC.

Negotiations began in earnest with Austria, Sweden, Finland and Norway in February 1993. Once under way, they proved extremely tortuous. The EFTA four, for all their initial craving for EC membership, turned out to be the toughest of negotiators. There was good reason for their hard-nosed posture, over and beyond what comes naturally in any diplomatic battle of wits among nations, for by then the winds of fortune had changed directions yet again.

The coming of the 1990s had transformed the EC into a place of upheaval with the traumas caused by German reunification, currency turmoil and severe recession. Much of the allure had gone out of even the single market, given so much uncertainty. Membership was still perceived as desirable by the EFTA four as a means of having a say in the Community's decision-making process. There was still interest in the longer-term growth prospects of a more closely integrated Europe. But it was no longer entry at any price.

Perceptions had undergone a reversal on the EU side as well, but in the opposite direction in its case. With the recession-induced drain on public sector finances everywhere, Germany's need to support its eastern *Länder*, and the increasing call on regional development-type transfers out of the EU budget, the arrival of new wealthy members had come to be seen as a welcome development. No more did the EU desire to maintain the calculated attempt to keep them at arm's length.

Thus protracted haggling began to unfold over such matters as the environment, social protection, agricultural and regional support, fishing, voting rights within the Council of Ministers and contributions to the EU budget. It took just over a year to work out elaborate compromise solutions for each of these emotive and politically-charged issues. Begun in February 1993, the negotiations were concluded in March 1994, but only to be rejected by the Norwegian people. The outcome of the Swedish referendum was also close, though it did come out in favour of accession.

The circumstances in which this enlargement took place will be bound to cast their shadow on developments into the next century. The three new members are no longer the starry-eyed EC gazers of the 1980s. They will monitor the direction European integration takes with close attention and make their demands heard. Many of those issues, for the moment covered by the carefully woven web of compromise, may emerge again at any time.

Even if the member states, new as well as old, prove capable of showing enough restraint so as to put aside the more distinctly individual grievances, the one issue which is most likely to resurface is the question of voting rules within the Council of Ministers. Specifically, the main issue of debate will be where qualified majority voting is involved. Since the current direction, much to the horror of the British, is to extend the qualified majority to an increasingly wider range of the Council's business in place of unanimity, the matter is of growing significance for all concerned. The crucial issue is that of the "blocking minority," that is the number of votes deemed necessary to strike down a proposal.

Before enlargement, that number was twenty-three out of a total of seventy-six votes, weighted to reflect the relative size of each member state. Within this voting structure, it was possible for two of the larger states, each with an allocation of ten votes, to combine forces with just one of the smaller states with three votes, to vote down a motion, even if it had the support of the nine other nations. For the larger nations, this was the next best thing to the one country veto ensured under unanimity, while to the smaller countries the formula would always appear to reflect the egotism of the powerful.

The question then, was how to adjust the blocking minority given the participation of the three new members. A technical matter, it would seem, easily resolved by allocating a proportionate number of votes to the newcomers and raising the blocking threshold accordingly. The post-enlargement formula would then be four votes to each of the new members, bringing the total to ninety and the blocking minority to twenty-seven.

Yet, even with this seemingly undebatable solution, it was Britain which chose to take issue. It objected strongly to the raising of the blocking minority. Never happy with the drift away from unanimity as the reigning principle in EU decision-making, it was adamant that its right of veto should not be further undermined. It found an unaccustomed ally in Spain, which likewise wished to keep the *status quo* intact. This was for fear of the northern influence growing too dominant within the Council of Ministers. On the basis of the existing blocking threshold, the three Latin nations of Spain, Portugal and Italy together could still prevent a majority of member states getting their way, but this would no longer be possible if the blocking minority was to be changed.

As with everything else, a compromise was reached at the time, according to which the blocking minority would indeed be raised to twenty-seven, but where twenty-three to twenty-six votes were cast against a motion, decision on the issue would be postponed for "a rational period." While this settled the dispute for the time being, a precise definition of what constitutes the rational period in question has been studiously avoided. The British see it as a virtual shelving of an issue once the old blocking threshold has been reached, while the other member states, by and large, regard the solution as providing a grace period in which a consensus may be sought. There will come a time when those unspoken differences have to be brought to light, amid, no doubt, even more paranoia than was the case initially. The 1996 intergovernmental conference on the Maastricht Treaty review is likely to be one such occasion. The 1996 IGC will be a forum in which all of the many potentially disruptive issues, barely papered over for the sake of keeping the integration process alive in the midst of pan-European recession, will have to be addressed. Niceties will have to give way to specifics once the conference is convened.

Another issue which is likely to raise tempers at the intergovernmental conference is one that is closely linked to the blocking minority question. It may arguably prove the more fundamentally divisive problem. This is the question of the actual number of votes allocated to each member state under the qualified majority procedure. With the Central and East European nations lining up in anticipation of the next phase of enlargement, the question of how to prevent a dominance of the weak must necessarily be placed on the agenda with considerable urgency.

Moreover, hidden beneath these immediate concerns is what could well turn out to be the most explosive question of all: the weighting of the German vote. The stated principle is that member states' voting rights should be weighted in line with their population. Yet at present Germany, France, Britain and Italy all hold an identical ten votes within the Council of Ministers, in spite of the increase in German population through reunification. The understanding at the time of reunification was that keeping the number of votes unchanged would be the transitionally wiser course to take, pending the 1996 review. Now that the 1996 review is just around the corner, time is running out on that transitional arrangement. Will France agree to a reallocation of votes that redresses the current imbalance? Will Germany insist on a readjustment, notwithstanding the distinct North-Eastern tilt that will become apparent in the Council of Ministers as a result?

The Way East

For better or for worse, the two Nordic states and Austria are now full members of the European Union. Now the time has come for enlargement to turn eastward. To this end, invitations were extended to six Central and Eastern European countries to be present at the Essen summit of December 1994. They were Hungary, Poland, the Czech Republic, Slovakia, Bulgaria and Romania, all of which are signatories to European Agreements, through which they are regarded as associate nations of the EU. These countries were promised at the Essen summit that preparations for their future accession would go ahead, albeit without any indication of the specific time scale involved.

In straightforward economic terms, the gains to be had from the EU's eastward enlargement are by no means beyond dispute. To be sure, the greater purchasing power that will emerge in Central and Eastern Europe as economic reform progresses should provide the EU member states with more markets and more growth opportunities. New investment frontiers will present themselves to EU manufacturers, as they consider setting up production facilities there. Battling against the very low cost producers of Central and Eastern Europe could prove to be the stimulus needed to facilitate, as in the words of *Growth, Competitiveness and Employment*, the ". . . strategy to improve competitiveness," so that ". . . Community industry could then concentrate on those areas where it possesses competitive advantages, i.e. high value-added products and services . . . ," which could result in "jobs being created mainly in highly specialised areas in sectors exposed to international trade."

Yet significant as those beneficial factors may be, they do not necessarily require the full integration of the region into the EU structure for them to be enjoyed. EU nations could avail themselves of the future growth momentum of their easterly neighbours just as well, without having to bear the costs and possible risks incurred by granting them full membership. It is possible for the rest of the world to benefit from the spectacular growth of dynamic Asia, without becoming involved in special regional integration arrangements with them. The EU's relationship with Central and Eastern Europe ought not to be any different.

There are, in fact, reasons other than simple economic gain for which eastward enlargement has to be sought. As the introduction to the Presidency Conclusions of the Essen summit puts it, "ensuring the lasting peace and stability of the European continent and neighbouring regions" is one such major concern which drives the EU's eastern extension. The peace and stability of the European continent is indeed critically linked to developments in the regions beyond the now non-existent Iron Curtain. In the immediate post-war years, it was the awareness of the need to ensure lasting peace between France and Germany which drove Europe towards unity. In the immediate post-war period, securing a stable Eastern Europe has come to acquire the same significance that establishing Franco-German harmony had forty years ago.

Nonetheless, the economic price to be paid for that stability may prove dangerously high. Understandably, there is concern within the EU over the possibility of an influx of cheap manufactures and an exodus of jobs as a result of eastward enlargement. For obvious reasons, these fears are more pronounced among the poorer member states. There is also the fear that support for regional development via the EU budget may not be as forthcoming as before, given the arrival of newcomers with urgent development needs of their own. While there are studies that indicate such concerns to be unfounded, anxieties of this kind are never easily banished by academic findings alone. Occasions could well arise where those member states who see themselves as most directly threatened feel compelled to resort to wage dumping, exchange rate dumping or both in self-defence. Bringing in the new Europeans could thus turn out to be the trigger that sets off currency warfare in Europe.

Moreover, there is the danger that the Franco-German harmony that Europe has been so much at pains to create and maintain thus far may become strained as a result of the EU's march eastward. Much as the need for stability in Central and Eastern Europe is a mutual concern of all EU member states, it is still primarily a German preoccupation. In a much-publicised paper presented by a CDU/CSU parliamentary group in the German Bundestag, the case is argued as follows:

Now that the East-West conflict has come to an end, a stable order must be found for the eastern half of the continent too. This is in the interest of Germany in particular since owing to its position, it would suffer the effects of instability in the East more quickly and directly than others. The only solution which will prevent a return to the unstable pre-war system . . . is to integrate Germany's Central and Eastern European neighbours into the (West) European post-war system . . . If (West) European integration were not to progress, Germany might be called upon, or be tempted by its own security constraints, to try to effect the stabilisation of Eastern Europe on its own and in the traditional way.[2]

Such reasoning has urged Germany to act as the prime driving force behind eastward enlargement, to the growing discomfiture of France, as well as its Mediterranean partners Spain and Italy. Germany played a major role in pushing forward the enlargement to bring in the Nordic countries and Austria, because this was the necessary step that had to be taken before the eastward enlargement could commence. Its aggressive taking of the initiative incurred the wrath of the Greeks who held the presidency of the Council of Ministers at the time. Spain also expressed unhappiness with the treatment it received from Germany during its negotiations over fishing rights with the Nordic states. At one point the German Foreign Minister, Klaus Kinkel, was heard saying that he would break the backs of the Spaniards to get an agreement. Other nations looked on with dismay at this show of German arrogance.

It was to appease the concerns of the Latin member states that, having established the need to prepare for the accession of Central and Eastern Europe, the Essen summit communiqué had to take note of the need to develop "in parallel the special relationship of the Union to its other neighbours, particularly the Mediterranean countries." To this end a new Mediterranean policy is being developed, whereby the EU will endeavour to assist political stabilisation and economic development in the Arab Middle East and North African regions along Mediterranean coastlines, and to establish a Euro-Mediterranean free trade zone.

Club Med

For Mediterranean EU members security in the Maghreb and Mashraq is of crucial importance, and the rising tide of Islamic fundamentalism is a legitimate cause of urgent concern. Ensuring political stability and economic progress in that region is the southern member states' protective shield against a torrent of migrants arriving from across the Mediterranean, as well as against "fundamentalist extremism, terrorism, drugs and organised crime" as the European Commission's communication on Euro-Mediterranean partnership puts it. In this sense, their position and that of Germany *vis-à-vis* Central and Eastern Europe have much in common.

From this perspective alone, there is ample reason for the EU to pay as much attention to its southern as well as north-eastern strategy. However, the Latin vs. German balance of power is also an undeniable underlying consideration, and it is this factor which facilitated the hasty endorsement of a new Mediterranean policy. While it appears as though the right balance has been struck for the moment, the longer-term implication of having explicitly acknowledged the existence of the two separate axes could prove hazardous for Europe. The Franco-German marriage begins to look increasingly less intimate and, more and more, like the image of fragile alliances among the princely families of the sixteenth and seventeenth centuries.

The CDU/CSU paper is significant in this regard, as are its bold statements on eastward enlargement. It scolds the French in remarkably harsh terms for their dithering over European union and their ambivalence regarding the Franco-German relationship. This is what the paper has to say on the subject:

. . . In France there are fears that the process of enlargement . . . could transform the Union into a loose grouping of states in which Germany might acquire far greater power and thus assume a dominant position. For France, therefore, the issue of deepening the Union prior to enlargement is of vital importance. Now that Germany is reunited . . . now that it can once again pursue an active foreign policy in the East . . . the old question of how to integrate a powerful Germany into European structures . . . assumes a new, if not in fact its real, meaning . . . It is important for Franco-German relations . . . that this question be addressed frankly . . . If Germany puts forward clear and unequivocal proposals, then France must make equally clear and unequivocal decisions. It must rectify the impression that, although it allows no doubt as to its basic will to pursue European integration, it often hesitates in taking concrete steps towards this objective – the notion of the unsurrenderable sovereignty of the 'Etat nation' still carries weight, although this sovereignty has long since become an empty shell . . .[3]

In many respects, the paper, with its candid language, is one of the clearest signs yet of the change that is taking place in the German position within the European Union. The once silent economic giant is in search of a political voice, with which to articulate whom it would like to see playing in its garden.

At a New Year press conference in 1994, Jacques Delors observed that, "The time has come to think of constructing a greater Europe." The time is certainly past when a handful of industrial nations could consider themselves as representing the European identity. That being said, the basic framework for a united Europe that was envisaged in the immediate post-war years is simply not equipped to handle the kind of geographical extension that is being discussed today. The original vessel was designed to contain just six countries, with, moreover, an already relatively high degree of economic homogeneity. It is verging on the absurd to assume that such a vessel can be used for a greater

Europe that aspires to an eventual twenty-five or even twenty-seven countries.

Which is precisely why the 1996 intergovernmental conference is being convened. European leaders are correct in their judgement that the EU's rules and institutions need to be reviewed and reformed in the light of recent developments. Yet the more it tries to adapt, the more it seems that the vessel suffers from new cracks spreading across its surfaces. There are limits to the expansion it can accommodate without falling apart. That breaking point will be severely tested as the intergovernmental conference progresses. There is nothing to ensure that the EU vessel will survive the test in one piece.

4–3 The Atlantic Alliance Adrift

Clinton's New Pacific Community

"The time has come for America to join with Japan and others in this region to create a New Pacific Community,"[4] said President Bill Clinton on 7 July 1993 in a speech delivered at Waseda University in Tokyo, with just a few hours to go before the opening of the G7 Tokyo summit meeting. He declared that such a New Pacific Community would "rest on a revived partnership between the United States and Japan, on progress towards more open economies and greater trade, and on support for democracy."

These words came as a great shock to Europe. The Waseda University speech was one which set the basic tone of Mr Clinton's approach to the summit meeting. It was also considered to be an important indicator of the foreign policy priorities of his administration. For such a statement to have contained the words "New Pacific Community," and to have stated so pointedly the significance that the bilateral relationship with Japan held for the United States, was cause for much consternation in the EU member states. What would become of the transatlantic relationship with Europe, now that American eyes had turned so ardently towards the Pacific and Asia? Having being voted into power on a platform of change, would the Clinton administration regard the Atlantic alliance as nothing more than a relic of the past generation? Could it be that the United States would now embark on the building of new economic ties and the development of a new security policy in which Europe had no place? Such fears seemed all the more pressing given that, on the day before Mr Clinton's Waseda University speech, US Secretary of State

Warren Christopher had remarked that Asia was now the most important region in the world for the United States.

Developments following the Tokyo summit appeared to endorse Europe's concerns. On 20 November the Asia-Pacific ECONOMI participants at the gathering were the United States, Japan, China, South Korea, Australia, New Zealand, Canada, Hong Kong, Taiwan, and the five members of the ASEAN excluding Malaysia (i.e. Brunei, Indonesia, the Philippines, Singapore and Thailand). Malaysia chose not to take part as a show of protest against American dominance. The summit meeting, nonetheless, included fourteen nations of great diversity. The agreements reached at the meeting pointed to the creation of an Asia-Pacific community. The progressive elimination of all barriers to trade and investment would be pursued and joint efforts would be made to solve outstanding regional and global economic issues, with the aim of securing better environmental conditions and sustainable economic growth.

When it was launched in 1989, the Asia-Pacific Economic Community (APEC) was nothing more than a forum for discussion regarding the possible strengthening of pan-Pacific ties. In Seattle it had begun to acquire the look of a regional community headed for closer integration. Not all the participating nations are agreed on its future direction. Many of the Asian members were openly wary of American dominance. Prime Minister Mahatir Mahamud of Malaysia expressed precisely such concerns by not turning up at all at the meeting. But such internal feuds were of little interest to the EU. For the EU member states, the alarming point was that America's interests and enthusiasm had turned resolutely towards the Asia-Pacific. The EU had hoped to be invited to the Seattle meeting as an observer, but had been turned down. This was only to be expected, just as the United States, Japan or members of the ASEAN would have discovered had it occurred to them to request observer status at a gathering of the EU. Nonetheless, being snubbed only added to the frustration of the Europeans.

Furthermore, the controversial NAFTA (North American Free Trade Agreement) bill had finally passed through the US House of Representatives just three days before the Seattle meeting, paving the way to the creation of a free trade area between the United States, Canada and Mexico. Mexico took part in the Seattle conference and was immediately endorsed as a member of APEC. Europe had to sit back and watch, while a vast economic space began to take shape before its eyes without any hope of the EU being able to take direct part in that development. Included in that space was East Asia, the fastest-growing region in today's world economy. And the United States was providing a link between that region and North America. The European sense of isolation was more than understandable.

Farewell New Atlanticism

The feeling of dismay might not have been quite so acute, had the European economy been in better shape at the time. Europe's attitude towards the United States tends very much to reflect its own internal degree of resilience. When things are going well, American overtures are interpreted as unsolicited meddling. This was very much its response to President Bush in 1989, when he made his call for a "New Atlanticism," emphasising the need to reconstruct the Atlantic alliance within the context of the post-cold war global order.

While Europe did not exactly cold-shoulder the proposal, it was by no means aglow with enthusiasm. At that time, the European Community had the single market in sight, coupled with the possibility of a whole new frontier opening up to its east, as economic reforms progressed in the former Communist countries. It was a period of rare hope and confidence for Europe. It had little time to concern itself with the United State's whims and fancies. Europe could get by on its own without any new Atlanticism.

There is little room for such complacency in today's Europe. Progress beyond the single market has proved to be much more uphill work than had been perceived. Even the single market itself has not functioned as the great dynamo of growth that was envisaged. The emergence of a new Pacific community could only add fuel to a pervading sense of uncertainty.

The United States, for its part, is no longer the US of 1989, when it was looking on with no small wonder at a Europe forging ahead with the single market programme, seemingly on the verge of a genuine era of renewed vigour and dynamism. At that time, it was the US which felt that it could ill-afford being left out in the cold. That sense of urgency is now gone. Even if the Bush administration had managed to hold onto power, the New Atlanticism would have, in all probability, been quietly dropped out of its agenda well before the G7 meeting in Tokyo.

Clinton goes to Europe

Even the timing of President Clinton's first visit to Europe seemed to symbolise the demotion that it had received in the United States' perceptions. He had waited until January 1994, a full year after taking office, to cross the Atlantic. His Asian trip and the launching of the New Pacific Community proposal had taken place six months earlier.

Nor was his maiden speech, once he had finally arrived there, one to provoke much excitement or warmth of feeling. It was, however, certainly awaited with much interest. Even though Mr Clinton's leadership qualities had, by then, been widely called into question for some time, he was still the first post-war generation United States President, and as such, how he meant to steer the United States' relationship with its oldest ally was something Europe did need to know. How to restructure the transatlantic relationship in line with the post cold war scheme of things, was a very large question mark hovering on the European horizon. To understand the American side of the solution, Europeans listened intently to Mr Clinton's words, addressed to them specifically for the first time.

The speech was delivered on 9 January in the Gothic hall of the Brussels Town Hall, to an audience of young European students. In it the President stated that he had "come here today to declare and to demonstrate that Europe remains central to the interests of the United States." For him, "the bonds that tie the United States and Europe are unique . . . the core of our security remains with Europe. That is why America's commitment to Europe's safety and stability remains as strong as ever."[5] There was nothing here that stepped beyond the acknowledgement of a friendship that went back a long way, an assurance that nothing had changed. It did not sound like an invitation to forge a new partnership in keeping with the dawning of a new era. Compared with the ringing tones in which the New Pacific Community was declared, the Brussels message to Europeans sounded distinctly low-key. Europe had not waited for a whole year to hear what amounted to nothing more than conventional courtesy.

Worse still, it would appear that Mr Clinton's eyes were focused not so much on the Atlantic alliance, but more on what lies beyond: developments in former Communist Europe and Russia. He pointed out that:

". . . we must know that we serve our own prosperity and our security by helping the new market economies of Europe's eastern half to thrive . . . wealthy nations cannot grow richer unless they have customers beyond their borders for their goods and their services . . . The United States has already eliminated many of our Cold War barriers to products from these countries. And all our nations must find more ways to do the same thing . . . We in the transatlantic community must commit ourselves to helping democracy succeed in all the former communist states that are Western Europe's immediate neighbours . . . Nowhere is democracy's success more important to us all than there and then in Russia."[6]

Having thus reiterated the significance of Russia and Eastern Europe for all he was worth, Mr Clinton went even further in a press conference held two days after the Brussels speech, where he said: "I came to Brussels in the hope of working with the leaders of Europe to build a broader and more integrated Europe."[7] He seemed almost to be saying that without a large-scale opening up toward the east, the whole idea of an integrated Europe had little meaning for him.

Defender of the Faith

The Atlantic alliance is a reflection of the cold-war era and its security requirements. As such it is more or less an historical inevitability that the relationship should be placed under strain today. In the cold-war climate, the existence of an internally cohesive Europe was indispensable to the United States for the obvious reasons of guarding against Communist encroachment. Successive post-war administrations invariably supported closer European integration as a matter of course from this perspective. On the other hand, had it not been for the security concerns, European integration would have been by no means something that the United States would have welcomed with open arms. The more self-sufficient and inward-looking the European economy became, the less chance American industry would have of penetrating its markets. Just as Europe feels threatened by NAFTA and APEC today, the United States of those years was always mindful of the potential loss that it was likely to incur as a result of European integration.

The European side did, indeed, wish to break gradually free from its immediate post-war dependence on the United States, and this was very much a part of the reason for promoting integration. Post-war rebuilding of Europe would not have been possible without the Marshall Plan, but once the initial hurdles of reconstruction had been negotiated successfully, the desire to step out from under the protective pinions of the US and to re-establish the European identity was quickly rekindled. In economic terms, it was feared that, unless Europe pulled together, American multinationals would come in and have a field day in their domestic markets. Charles de Gaulle was the torchbearer of this anti-Americanism. He suspected Britain of being a Trojan horse that had been sent in by the Americans to spy out the land. This was one reason why he was adamant that Britain should not be allowed to join the Community.

The Americans were thus placed in the paradoxical position of wishing to see closer integration in Western Europe so as to secure a bulwark against the enemy beyond the Iron Curtain, while at the same time fearing the economic consequences of a too independent-minded Europe. But this was a dilemma that the United States simply had to learn to live with. So long as the Iron Curtain was a feature of life on the European continent, the Atlantic alliance was of supreme importance and the US must not stand in the way of the Community's pursuit of closer integration. Indeed there were even occasions where the United States persuaded the reluctant British to take a positive view of the Common Market.

European Ideals of Union Challenged

While the fate of the New Pacific Community is anything but certain, it cannot be denied that NAFTA and APEC together constitute something of a large antithesis to Europe's ideals of unity and integration.

As regional economic integrations go, NAFTA and APEC can be said to represent everything that the EU is not. NAFTA aspires literally to be a free trade area, a form of integration that Europe turned its back on at the start. The question remains whether at some point NAFTA might not consider venturing into the realms of customs union and even monetary union. That, however, is not the direction that is being pursued at the moment. On the contrary, it looks as though a conscious decision was made to avoid the internal strife that has come to plague the EU by keeping things simple. Indeed, American observers are fond of pointing out that regional integration should never venture beyond the free trade area if maximum economic gains are to be had at minimal political and social risk.

The validity of such statements remains to be seen. It could be that, as Ross Perot was fond of pointing out, NAFTA will become the vehicle through which a large-scale exodus of employment opportunity from the United States into Mexico takes place. Whether the American economy actually has the internal resilience to avail itself fully of the opportunities presented by a vastly wider market is also an open question: the American economy is no longer as young an economy as it would like to think. These elements of uncertainty notwithstanding, the fact remains that a typically non-EU form of regional integration has found shape in NAFTA, providing an alternative route to possibly greater economic gain.

As for APEC, its future is arguably a great deal more precarious than that of NAFTA. On the other hand, it has one overwhelming advantage in that it encompasses the one area of the world where rapid economic growth is guaranteed for some time to come. Gone are the days when leading industrial economies provided the world with growth momentum. The growth centre has shifted to those very countries that form the core group of APEC. Regional groupings that consist of economies with dynamic growth potential tend to manifest a self-perpetuating inward pull: precisely the element that is missing in today's Europe. The United States has embarked on an effort to harness that cohesive energy to its own growth mechanics. Whether the US will succeed in this venture is a topic beyond the scope of this book, but the challenge posed by the emergence of APEC is something that the EU cannot afford to ignore.

The Atlantic alliance has come up against the New Pacific Community and the European Union is being challenged by NAFTA and APEC. At a time of declining solidarity within, new ideas are flowering without. Europe needs to rise to the occasion with alternative ideas of its own. But this it cannot do, so long as it remains entrapped within the confines of the Maastricht blueprint.

---

[1] *The Financial Times*. 31 December 1993

[2] *Reflections on European Policy*. Document presented by the CDU/CSU parliamentary group in the German Parliament (Bundestag), text as published in *Europe*, No. 1895/96. 7 September 1994

[3] *ibid.*

[4] *The Times*. 8 July 1993

[5] *Europe*, No. 1868. 14 January 1994

[6] *ibid.*

[7] *ibid.*

5

In Search of New Heroes

The curtain falls on *Götterdämmerung* with the funeral of Siegfried. The hero's death purges the world of the hatred and confrontation that had so plagued it as a result of the greed and folly of the gods. Yet as Siegfried's funeral pyre burns the heavens, and Valhalla, once believed to be indestructible, is consumed in flames, we are not shown precisely what lies beyond the collapse of the old world. It is now time to contemplate what that future might be for a Europe whose twentieth-century gods, giants and dwarfs appear increasingly less capable of sustaining a harmonious universal order.

The Four Relevant Questions

Four questions would seem to need addressing, if one's vision is to penetrate the twilight of the twentieth century and focus on a possible twenty-first century lease of life for Europe. One is the issue of economic viability: will closer integration remain the key that will continue to open doors to greater and lasting prosperity for the peoples of Europe in the twenty-first century? Secondly and co-relatedly, how feasible is it for the Europe of today to retain the goal of monetary union with all the requirements of cohesion and convergence that this entails? Thirdly, is it the pull of economic gain, or the logic of politics and international relations, which takes fundamental precedence as a motive for closer union among peoples? Was Walter Hallstein, first President of the EEC Commission, revealing the ultimate wisdom when he remarked that "the Community's business is not business but politics"?

The fourth and last, although most certainly not least, of the questions is what the rising internal tide of regionalism within the Community means. When one talks of regionalism within the context of economic integration in Europe or elsewhere, the notion of regional blocs, with its underlying connotation of protectionism, is apt to be of predominant concern. Observe the recurrent fears voiced of "fortress Europe" in discussions relating to the single market. As worrisome as the prospect of a fortress Europe may be, however, it seems to be an entirely different brand of regionalism that is spreading across Europe these days.

"*Secessione!*" cries Umberto Bossi in the foothills of the Italian Alps. The Walloons and the Flemings ponder the prospect of a complete separation, now that Belgium has officially become a federal state rather than a unified kingdom. The Catalan cry for greater autonomy grows stronger by the day. The paradoxical outcome of German unification has been the even greater self-awareness of what were already considerably independent-minded *Länder*. While a feature of European history over many centuries has been that of regional entities aspiring to establish their own separate political, economic, social and cultural identity, this voice of separatism seems to have acquired a new prominence as we approach the turn of this particular century.

This has as much to do with the prosaic issue of money as with the virtuous passion for independence. In the midst of the worst Europe-wide recession since the 1930s, Flanders began to wonder why it must subsidise Wallonia out of the pockets of its own citizens. Northern Italy would like to keep its wealth for itself, rather than see it squandered away by its spendthrift and corrupt brethren of the *Mezzogiorno*. Industrious Catalonia feels entitled to invest the fruits of its efforts for its own benefit, not in support of infrastructure-building in the poorer south. Income transfer via the state is all very well at times of expanding overall wealth: when the pie stops growing, the willingness to share becomes distinctly limited. The yearning for self-determination becomes all the more urgent in adverse economic circumstances.

Another form of resistance against central control can be seen in the case of Denmark's initial refusal to ratify the Maastricht Treaty. "If you can't join them, beat them," remarked the then Danish Foreign Minister, Uffe Ellemann-Jensen, on 26 June 1992, as he received news of Denmark's victory over Germany in the European football championship finals. This was three weeks after the Danish 'no' vote in the Maastricht referendum and also the day on which the European

Council met in Lisbon. As Mr Elleman-Jensen's further comment that the Danish team's achievement "shows small states can win. And Europe needs small states" implies, the underlying fear of falling under the dominance of the larger states is a concern that can only grow as higher levels of political and economic integration are sought. And the desire to beat rather than join is surely magnified if greater interdependence does not bring with it greater wealth, but rather the rapid transmission of recessionary pressures from one member state to another.

All this leads back to the first question of Europe's ability to generate growth. There was, of course a time when the growth effect of closer integration was not in doubt. The years between 1958 and 1967 were precisely such a time, when the six original members of the Community benefited greatly from the mutual abolition of import tariffs and the adoption of common external tariffs in the process of creating a customs union. In so doing, the member states were able to break free from the growth constraints imposed on them by the limited size of their respective domestic markets. Together they enjoyed a golden era of export-led growth, which was impressive enough to give the Euro-wary British second thoughts about their splendid isolation and make them make their first tentative move to join rather than beat the Continental team. But all this happened when the Community was in its adolescence. With middle age setting in, today's Europe could hardly be expected to perform in the same manner. A health-endangering dose of inflationary policy steroids would be needed to make a re-run of the 1960s possible.

The single most problematic issue for today's Europe is that it can no longer count on the driving force of a West German locomotive to keep the growth momentum going. So long as the effort to support the eastern side continues to drain western Germany of its macroeconomic resilience, it cannot be relied on to play the erstwhile engine role for the EU as a whole. While the most recent recession can now be considered as over, the longer-term ability of Germany to be the central axis around which the European growth machine rotates is questionable at best. Nor is there much likelihood that the trans-European infrastructure projects envisaged can provide a permanent replacement for the presence of a healthy economy endowed with the internal ability to generate growth.

The ERM: A Lost Cause

Given these circumstances, the difficulties attached to aiming for a currency union at this point is almost self-evident. The current state of the ERM is a graphic illustration of the underlying weakness of a regime of quasi-fixed parities, that centres around a single national currency. Such a system is, by nature, unilaterally dependent on the economic health of the key currency nation for survival. If anything goes wrong in that country, either in terms of the underlying macroeconomic situation or faulty policy management, stability of the system itself is instantly undermined.

In this sense, the ERM and the dollar standard regime of the Bretton Woods system have precisely the same characteristics. The only difference between the two, which is certainly intriguing if not as fundamental as it appears on first inspection, is that while the dollar standard went into self-destruct as a result of the inflationary policies of the United States, it was Germany's monetary austerity in the face of unification-induced inflationary pressures that brought about the ERM's demise.

During the United States' reign as the global key currency nation, the rest of the world suffered chronically from the inflationary consequences of the excess dollar overhang. So long as the US felt no compunction in forcing other nations to accept debts denominated in its own currency and they had no alternative but to acquiesce, the world was at the mercy of American monetary licence. There were limits, however, to how far even a reigning key currency nation could go, and in the end the United States was forced to abrogate in favour of a freely floating exchange rate system. Conversely, the presence of the D-Mark as key currency came to be the cause of a persistent deflationary bias in the macroeconomic fabric of Europe.

Interesting enough, it was just such a situation which was anticipated with concern as the Bretton Woods system came into effect. The rest of the world feared that one and all would become so indebted to the Americans that an acute shortage of dollars would become a serious constraint to growth momentum outside the United States. Focusing on this concern, John Maynard Keynes pointed out that Bretton Woods was a system which placed the burden of macroeconomic adjustment unilaterally on nations that register balance of payments deficits. As such, he maintained that the arrangement was at odds with its stated aim of enhancing growth and employment.

In reflection of such concerns, the IMF Treaty enshrines what is known as the "scarce currency" clause, whereby a nation which runs a large and persistent surplus in its balance of payments would either have to mend its ways in the management of its domestic economy, or face retribution in the form of import barriers set up against it by its trading partners. The provision was seen as a safeguard against dollar shortages, and it can only be considered the greatest of ironies that in the end, what the world economy suffered from was a persistent over-supply of the currency.

A somewhat transformed descendent of the "scarce currency" clause has found its way into the ERM in the shape of its "divergence indicator." This is the ratio of how far a currency's market exchange rate has diverged from its central rate against the ECU, set against the maximum degree of fluctuation allowed by the stipulated bands around parity. By aligning currencies according to their distance from the central rate, regardless of the direction in which they had deviated from parity, it was thought that the indicator would eliminate the element of asymmetry in the system, so that undue adjustment burdens would not fall on the weaker currencies. It is of some interest that once again it was the British, this time represented by the then Chancellor of the Exchequer, Denis Healey, which insisted on the adoption of this safeguard against asymmetry in favour of the strong currency nation.

In practice, the indicator itself has had little if any of the hoped for effect of imposing policy adjustments on Germany when the D-Mark appreciated against other currencies. The "scarce currency" nation within the ERM was not about to have its economic management censored through such flimsy devices. Moreover, times have moved on and it is now open to question whether, and to what extent, the D-Mark will remain a scarce currency. As it confronts the difficulties brought about by reunification, German economic policy seems tantalisingly poised between maintaining the stringent pursuit of price stability at its masthead, and succumbing to the twin-deficit solution adopted by the United States. If it goes the way of the latter, history will repeat itself in that a currency whose scarcity had been feared in reality plagues the world with its ubiquitousness. However improbable this sounds in the light of past record, the extent of the loss of equilibrium that has been visited on the German economy by reunification should not be underestimated.

Wherefore, the Single Currency?

In any event, the first-among-equals system of fixed exchange rates has been tested and seen to fail with the Bretton Woods experiment. There was no reason to assume that the ERM would fare any better. All the more reason, it would be argued, to move promptly toward a fully-fledged economic and monetary union. The problem with this line of reasoning is that it does not explain why such a union should take place at all. A single currency would eliminate exchange rate risk, would make it possible for travellers to make a round trip of the EU without having to suffer huge losses at every stop they make at a *bureau de change*: these are perfectly legitimate points in favour of a single currency. That being said, these oft-cited benefits of monetary union only take account of the currency's function as a transaction medium.

Embodied in the value of a currency is the purchasing power of an entire economy. Relative strengths and weaknesses of various national currencies reflect the positions that those nations hold in the hierarchy of economic performance. In principle, entities that share a common single currency should be equals in terms of their purchasing power. This principle was consciously ignored at the time of German reunification, the price of which was massive unemployment in the eastern *Länder* which had to be compensated for with large-scale income transfers from the west.

It is rightly argued that economic convergence must precede the adoption of a single currency. This, it is said, shall be achieved by nations adhering to the convergence criteria of the Maastricht Treaty. Yet is the alignment of a handful of statistics testimony enough to justify the formulation of a single currency domain, among national economies of vastly differing sizes and characteristics? This apart, a more fundamental problem with this approach is that it stands the argument on its head. Economies come to share a common currency because there is relative convergence and homogeneity among them. There is no reason why they should be forced to converge for the sake of moving to a single-currency system. It is the dog that wags the tail, not the tail that wags the dog.

Moreover, since perfect convergence is in any event impossible to achieve, conversion rates reflecting relative purchasing power will have to be allotted to the participating economies at the time that monetary union takes place. This would have to be the case, bar the unlikely event that the German example is followed and a one-to-one conversion is applied indiscriminately. Those conversion rates will determine the post-monetary union value of peoples' incomes, savings and assets. As such, they are sure to become a bone of the most ferocious contention, however they are derived, be it through the irrevocable fixing of exchange rates or otherwise.

It may be argued that since peoples' debts and the general level of prices will also be affected, nothing will change. Yet these are technicalities that still do not answer the ultimate simple question: to what end monetary union? The costs involved in holding together a single currency area are large, as no doubt any national government is only too keenly aware. The United States is perhaps the most prominent case in point. Its twin deficits are the price it has had to pay to maintain a single currency union comprising of fifty immensely diverse states. What economic convergence cannot achieve has to be secured through income transfer, once again as German monetary unification has graphically illustrated. Adoption of a single currency is not merely a matter of coinage. One currency has to mean one monetary policy, a single set of interest rates applied to rich and poor, the thriving and ailing alike. If matters are left to run their course, the rich will become richer and the poor will become poorer. Should this be allowed to happen? Or should the impact of uniform monetary management be softened by other means such as subsidies or special interest rate relief? The former would threaten social cohesion, the latter is the road to an EU version of the twin deficits. Why risk all this to introduce a single currency where none has existed, and without which economic activity takes place with no major distortions of a critically damaging nature.

Political Anachronism

There are times when such economic reasoning has to give way to political considerations. At times justifiably, at others not. In both cases, economics will take its revenge. German monetary unification was a political necessity which was virtually incontestable at the time. This did not make the subsequent economic costs any less burdensome. The politics of containing Germany governs France's *franc fort* policy, and it has paid dearly for its incorrigibility.

The question then is whether or not a convincing case can be made today that a European Union is politically worth defending and nurturing at all economic costs. At the time of the 1948 Congress of Europe, it was indeed apt to say: "My counsel to Europe can be given in a single word: 'Unite' "[1] as did Winston Churchill in the foreword to the proceedings of that meeting. Avoiding yet another disastrous war in Europe was certainly an overwhelmingly important aim to pursue through integration, even if there had been no accompanying economic gains. The ECSC proved to be a highly effective device in the rebuilding of Europe's post-war industrial underpinnings. But the willingness to pool national resources under common management stemmed from a determination to avoid, at all costs, tensions remounting between France and Germany.

That the ECSC member states lost no time in contemplating the formulation of a European Defence Community as their next step, is clear indication of the strong political motivation behind the integration process of the time. Aborted as it was by parliamentary resistance in France, that such a proposal should have been made at so early a point in post-war history shows how irrevocably linked the pursuit of closer integration was to the political desire for lasting peace in Europe. Moreover, the political significance of an integrated western Europe took on new dimensions as the Cold War structure matured. Member states felt the need to join forces against possible threats from beyond the Iron Curtain. The United States was an avid supporter of such team spirit.

In that era when the post-war global order was in the very process of taking shape, the political case for pursing ever-closer integration within Europe was easy to justify. Yet those days are long past, and the immediate post-war framework is no more. Important as it remains to prevent the outbreak of conflict, does the construction of a European Union have the same legitimacy as a means to that end today as it did in days gone by? History has now entered an entirely new dimension, and the time has come to ask whether the logic, that had once overwhelmingly endorsed greater integration in Europe, might not be turning into something of an anachronism.

No Single Currency, No Single Market

That monetary union is an increasingly elusive moving target has come to be acknowledged by a great many more people than was the case previously. On the other hand, the single market is more or less unanimously hailed as a great achievement which will survive even the possible failure of monetary union to materialise. Indeed, the achievement is a formidable one, but as to its future, an unqualified cheer may possibly be a little premature.

The question is whether, in fact, the single market can function to its fullest effect without a single currency. So long as exchange rate volatility remains, a genuine single market cannot be said to exist, however much tariffs are abolished, border controls removed, or technical standards unified. In this respect, it would in actual fact seem more appropriate to regard monetary union not as the next step that comes after the completion of a single market, but rather as the precondition to a functioning single market. This is not an advocacy of monetary union. The point is that where the conditions are not ripe for monetary union, nor is there the likelihood of a single market being established in the precise sense of the term.

Past record would seem to vindicate this view, for it was invariably at times of relative currency stability that European integration has made the most noticeable progress. Take the period 1958 to 1967, when the formation of the customs union marched forward ahead of schedule. The Bretton Woods system was still intact at the time: exchange rates were fixed against the dollar, and that was the end of that. Europe may have had to fret over the shortage of its dollar reserves, but there was no room for exchange rate relationships among the Community member states to hinder intra-EC trade in any way. The single market programme was also launched at a time of great calm among European currencies. The ERM had become the epitome of stability, with parity realignments few and far between. The dollar standard had been replaced by the D-Mark standard. Community member states could sail on into the single market without losing sleep over fears of exchange rate risk. To the ERM participants of the time, it may well have felt as though they were already taking part in a monetary union in all but name.

Circumstances have since changed beyond all recognition. The European Monetary Institute is in place, and not a day passes without some speculation over the timing of the single currency's introduction adorning the pages of the financial press. Yet the reality of the European currency market is a shambles. The ERM is no longer a mechanism that can either enhance or maintain exchange rate stability, and the D-Mark can barely tolerate the key currency role. This is not an environment in which a single market, however borderless it is in other respects, can thrive. Year-one of the single market may have been 1993, but with its unstable foundations there are very real doubts about its longevity.

Regions to the Fore

What is to be the shape of Europe in the twenty-first century? Multi-track, multi-speed, variable geometry, concentric circles, overlapping circles, *à la carte*, *table d'hôte*: the list of ideas currently in vogue reads like an elaborate exercise in allegory. None of them sound totally convincing. None seem capable of setting Europe free from the preoccupations and constraints of a passing age. The underlying conflict between political necessity and economic reality, the re-emergence of a unified Germany and the dislodging of the balance of power that this has given rise to: these are issues that ideas rooted in the post-war era essentially cannot address.

The Europe of concentric circles would seem to be the preferred French option, provided that France and Germany together form the core of the structure. A representative of the CNPF (Conseil National du Patronat Français) once pointed out that the ideal structure for Europe would look like one of those wooden Russian dolls that open up to reveal successively smaller versions of itself, until finally you arrive at a tiny core figurine. The idea is that the outer layers of the union may take whatever guises or sizes that is most fitting at each respective level, so long as there lies at the centre of it all a hard core of stable monetary and economic union, however small it may be. The metaphor is a clever one. Yet one wonders what the gentleman would have said if the core figure that pops out has only Helmut Kohl's face on it. Chancellor Kohl's face may not spell that much of a disaster after all, given his commitment to the Franco-German alliance. But what if it is of some other German leader less committed to the European Union and more inclined to look eastward? That could surely not be acceptable to France.

Europe *à la carte* lies at the furthermost end of the spectrum in relation to the Europe of concentric circles. Since no meaningful deepening of integration can be expected to take place according to this scenario, there would be no question of sealing Germany into a tightly-woven net of interlocking politico-economic relationships, which is what the French aim for. Germany will be left to roam free, perhaps even going on to establish a D-Mark currency area all its own. This is France's nightmare, against which it has been prepared to do battle even to the point of self-strangulation with the *franc fort*. It looks, however, as though it is beginning to lose both the battle and the war.

An alternative answer may just possibly lie in the resurgence of internal regionalism that was discussed earlier. By introducing the

concept of subsidiarity into the Maastricht Treaty, Europe may have
opened up something of a Pandora's Box. The official view is that
subsidiarity only extends to states and does not apply to regions within
states. But the representatives of those regions seem to pay no heed to
such pronouncements. And, indeed, by setting up the Committee of
Regions as an official Community institution, even the authors of the
Maastricht Treaty seem to acknowledge implicitly that subsidiarity
cannot be kept exclusively in the State vs. Community domain
of conflict.

It was surely a contradiction in terms to insert the notion of
subsidiarity into the Maastricht Treaty. The Maastricht Treaty is, after
all, a document setting out the blueprint for closer integration, while
subsidiarity is quintessentially a devolutionist concept. It speaks much
of the waning allure of the European Construction, when such
fundamental inconsistencies have to be endured in order to quell doubts
and to convince the suspicious.

From the Pandora's Box of subsidiarity may emerge forces of radical
separatism and fragmentation. Giving rein to such forces may lead to
chaos. Yet chaos is a great deal more creative than struggling to
maintain a stifling and outmoded *status quo*. The avid quest for
regional identity is virtually the only, totally unaccounted for, factor
that has emerged in the period between the signing of the Treaties of
Rome and today. That regional issues should rise to prominence was
certainly not in the masterplan of the founding fathers of the Union.
On the other hand, monetary union was already envisaged as a distant
but ultimate goal, even in the initial stages of the Community's
travails, as was indeed political union. As such, both are already
notions of a past era. But internal regionalism is not. It is a notion of
this time, the aspiration of a new age. Or rather, one that was obliged
to take the back seat in the post-war era, but is now rediscovering its
rightful place on the European stage.

It may be that existing states have simply become too large for
healthy competition or as creators of greater wealth. If the European
Construction can provide a space in which the regional performers are
able to unleash their talents, then the European drama of the twenty-
first century has the possibility of becoming a truly exciting one.
Europe needs competition within to revive it. Threading together a
collection of maturing economies and foisting a single currency upon
them is not going to make that possible. The convergence criteria are
like the innkeeper who has only one bed so chops the lodger's feet off

if they protrude from it, or stretches him with pulleys if he is too short for it. Either way, much pain and no gain. Economic integration has to be market-driven to have a good chance of success. That element was alive in the Europe of the 1950s. Today it is most dynamically alive in the East Asian economies, which form a vital part of the APEC grouping. If the latent energies of the regions within the EU can be allowed to manifest themselves, and could be utilised in such a way that they contribute to the return of healthy competition, market driven cohesion could indeed be revived in today's Europe.

Let's Have More Currencies

And what of the impact of growing on monetary union? The answer could well be the increase in the number of European currencies, rather than the merger of existing currencies into one single common currency. A little far-fetched perhaps, but why not? If integration is to be market-driven, this is a good way to start. At least none of the costly income transfers would be needed any longer. And it could, after all, prove to be an alternative route to the single currency. Former British Chancellor of the Exchequer, Nigel Lawson, once proposed the idea of competing currencies: allow all the existing currencies to circulate throughout the EU, then the competition among those currencies would eventually drive out all the weaker ones, and Europe would be left with a single currency that no one has any reservations or compunctions about accepting. The general standard of economic performance as well as policy management would rise in the process, since all the participating nations would work hard to make their own currency the most desirable choice for everyone else. The underlying logic of the idea was inherited by the hard ECU proposal of John Major's government. Whether or not a complete reversal of Gresham's law will actually occur is somewhat open to doubt, but the process would certainly be market-driven and involve less pain than seeking accommodation with the Maastricht innkeeper.

Minerva's Messenger

Twilight seems, indeed, to cast deep gloom on turn-of-the-century Europe. Yet there is hope still for, as Hegel would have us know, Minerva's owl of wisdom takes flight at dusk. It is in the demise of an era that the next age finds life. From Johann Simon Mayr, Gaetano Donizetti's mentor and whose Bavarian Illuminati took the owl of wisdom as its symbol, to Karl Marx, who scrutinised and questioned the existing system as none before him had done, those in search of a new era become fascinated by Minerva's messenger.

The courage to discard the old garments of a passing age will call forth new heroes. On the other hand, if all that the European Union can do is to cling to the Valhalla of Maastricht, built according to the basic architecture of the post-war framework, only endless night can lie beyond the twilight of the twentieth century.

---

[1] Soledad Garciá (Ed.). *European Identity and the Search for Legitimacy.* London. 1993

References

Ash, T.G. 1993. *In Europe's Name: Germany and the Divided Continent*. Jonathan Cape, London.

Bank of England. *Bank of England Quarterly Bulletin*, Volume 32, No. 3, August 1992; No. 4, November 1992; Volume 33, No 1, February 1993; Volume 34, No. 3, August 1994, London.

Campbell, E.S. 1989. *Germany's Past and Europe's Future: The Challenges of West German Foreign Policy*. Pergamon-Brassey's International Defense Publishers Inc., New York.

CDU/CSU Parliamentary Group in the German Parliament (Bundestag). 1994. *Reflections on European Policy*. Europe. No. 1895/96. 7 September 1994, Bonn.

Colchester, N. and Buchan, D. 1990. *Europe Relaunched: Truths and Illusions on the Way to 1992*. The Economist Books, Hutchinson Business Books Ltd., London.

Commission on Employment Issues in Europe. 1989. *A Programme for Employment in the 1990s*. Pergamon Press, Oxford.

Conseil National du Patronat Français. 1993. *Observations du CNPF Sur les Dysfonctionnements du Marché Intérieur European*, CNPF, Paris.

Cooper, R.N. 1968. *The Economics of Interdependence: Economic Policy in the Atlantic Community*. McGraw-Hill Book Company, New York.

Cowie, H. and Pinder, J. 1993. *A Recovery Strategy for Europe*. Federal Trust, London.

Crawford, M. 1993. *One Money for Europe? The Economics and Politics of Maastricht*. Macmillan Press, London.

De Grauwe, P. and Papademos, L. 1990. *The European Monetary System in the 1990s*. Longman, New York.

Duff, A. (Ed.). 1993. *Subsidiarity within the European Community*. Federal Trust, London.

Garciá, S. (ed.). 1993. *European Identity and the Search for Legitimacy*. Pinter Publishers Ltd., London.

George, S. 1990. *An Awkward Partner: Britain in the European Community*. Oxford University Press, Oxford.

Giao, D.D.T. 1994. *Le Système Monétaire International et L'Europe: Du Sterling Standard à l'Union Économique et Monétaire: Croissance, développement, Intégration, Équilibre*. Les Editions Sciences et Techniques Humaines, Paris.

Giavazzi, F., Micossi, S., and Miller, M. 1988. *The European Monetary System*. Cambridge University Press, Cambridge.

Göbbel, B., Moecke, H.J. and Rubbra, D. 1991. *Doing Business in the Five New German Laender*. The Federal Office of Foreign Trade Information (BFAI), Cologne.

Gold, M. 1993. *The Social Dimension: Employment Policy in the European Community*. Macmillan Press, London.

Goodhart, D. 1994. *The Reshaping of the German Social Market*. Institute of Public Policy Research, London.

Hare, P. and Simpson, L. 1993. *British Economic Policy: A Modern Introduction*. Harvester Wheatsheaf, Hertfordshire.

Harrison, M., Hayward, J., Howorth, J., Machin, H., Wright, V., and Stevens, A. 1993. *De Gaulle to Mitterrand: Presidential Power in France*. Hurst & Company, London.

Kishigami, S. and Tanaka, T. (Ed.). 1989. *The EC 1992 Handbook*. The Japan Times, Tokyo.

Kuper, S. 1994. *Football Against the Enemy*. Orion, London.

Lawson, N. 1992. *The View From No. 11*. Bantam Press, London.

Leonardi, R. (ed.). 1993. *The Regions and the European Community: The Regional Response to the Single Market in the Underdeveloped Areas*. Frank Cass & Co. Ltd., London.

Leonardi, R. and Nanetti, R. Y. 1990. *The Regions and European Integration: The Case of Emilia-Romagna*. Pinter Publishers Ltd., London.

Lippert, B. and Stevens-Strohmann, R. 1993. *German Unification and EC Integration: German and British Perspectives*. The Royal Institute of International Affairs, Pinter Publishers Ltd., London.

Marsh, D. 1994. *Germany and Europe: The Crisis of Unity*. Heinemann, London.

Miall, H. 1993. *Shaping the New Europe*. The Royal Institute of International Affairs, Pinter Publishers Ltd., London.

Minford, P. 1992. *The Cost of Europe*. Manchester University Press, New York.

Minikin, R. 1993. *The ERM Explained: A Straightforward Guide to the Exchange Rate Mechanism and the European Currency debate.* Kogan Page, London.

OECD. *OECD Economic Outlook*, No. 52, December 1992; No. 53, June 1993; No. 54, December 1993; No. 55, June 1994. OECD Publications, Paris.

Petacco, A. 1993. *La Principessa del Nord: La misteriosa vita della dama del Risorgimento: Cristina di Belgioioso.* Arnoldo Mondadori Editore, Milan.

Pinder, J. 1991. *European Community: The Building of a Union.* Oxford University Press, Oxford.

Putnam, R. D. 1993. *Making Democracy Work – Civic Traditions in Modern Italy.* Princeton University Press, Princeton.

Smith, M. and Woolcock, S. 1993. *The United States and the European Community in a Transformed World.* The Royal Institute of International Affairs, Pinter Publishers Ltd., London.

Spierenburg, D. and Poidevin, R. 1994. *The History of the High Authority of the European Coal and Steel Community: Supranationality in Operation.* Weidenfeld and Nicolson, London.

Takahashi, J. and Hama, N. 1992. *Doru wa Yomigaeruka (Can the Dollar Recover?).* Nihon-hyoronsha, Tokyo.

Temperton, P. 1993. *The European Currency Crisis: What Chance Now for a Single European Currency?* Probus Publishing Company, Cambridge.

Thatcher, M. 1993. *The Downing Street Years.* Harper Collins, London.

Tsoukalis, L. 1993. *The New European Economy: The Politics and Economics of Integration,* Second Revised Edition. Oxford University Press, New York.

Turner, H. A. Jr. 1992. *Germany from Partition to Reunification.* Yale University Press, New Haven & London.

Urwin, D. W. 1968. *Western Europe Since 1945: A Political History.* Longman, New York.

Index

Recent Volumes of Related Interest

SMALL IS POWERFUL
The Future as if People Really Mattered
by John Papworth

"This book could well do for the Nineties what Schumacher's *Small is Beautiful* did for the sixties. It is completely revolutionary . . . it will meet dogged resistance from the establishment and from nearly everyone else; but the world really needs this message, and unless someone can give it, and most of us receive it, my grandchildren are in for a miserable time."

> **John Seymour**, Author of *The Complete Book of Self Sufficiency* and co-author of *Blueprint for a Green Planet*

CREATIVE COMPARTMENTS
A Design for Future Organisation
by Gerard Fairtlough

"Too many of us are macho managers who regard busy-ness as an end in itself. We deny ourselves time for reflection. We fail to assimilate ideas like those which Fairtlough collected on his own long journey – during which he was strongly influenced by contacts and reading and face-to-face discussion with colleagues and gurus."

> **Professor Sir Douglas Hague**, Chairman, Oxford Strategic Leadership Programme

RESOURCES FOR THE FUTURE
An International Annotated Bibliography for the 21st Century
by Alan J. Mayne

"So much wisdom from so many well-informed thinkers, supported by so many publishers – one is compelled to reflect that there is yet hope for a saner world."
Fourth World Review

"A valuable resource focused on the burgeoning literature dealing with futures from several perspectives – environmental, economic, political, social, technological, and conceptual . . . Recommended for all undergraduates and research-level libraries."
Choice

GROUPWARE IN THE 21ST CENTURY
Computer Supported Co-operative Working Towards the Millennium
Edited by Peter Lloyd

"Unlike many books covering new technology developments, this book is distinctive in that it places emphasis on the processes and people issues . . . I would comment this book to lanners who want to gain an appreciation of what groupware is all about."
Long Range Planning: The Journal of International Strategic Management

"Anyone who wants to know more about the future of technology and group processes will find this book provides them with something to think about."
Lotus SmartNotes

THE FORESIGHT PRINCIPLE
Cultural Recovery in the 21st Century
by Richard Slaughter

"richly contributes to the deep thought we must all partake in as we struggle for a new society"
> **Professor Lester Milbrath**, State University of New York,
> Author of *Envisioning a Sustainable Future*

"clearly written, accessible . . . an important milestone in the continuing emergence of the field of futures studies"
> **Professor Wendell Bell**, Yale University

"This book fills a deep need in today's cultural transitions and confusions – expanding the contexts for further human development . . . This book will serve to excite interest in the whole field of futures research and its still budding potential for the next stages of human development."
> **Hazel Henderson**, Author of *Creating Alternative Futures* and *Paradigms in Progress*

VITALITY AND RENEWAL
A Manager's Guide for the 21st Century
by Colin Hutchinson

"When you enter an unknown country you don't want several guidebooks giving you conflicting directions. You want one in which different perspectives are resolved. That is what Colin Hutchinson provides in Vitality and Renewal, as the New Industrial Revolution begins to dawn."
> **John Davis**, formerly Chairman and MD of Shell Composites Limited, author of *Greening Business*

THE END OF THE FUTURE
The Waning of the High-Tech World
by Jean Gimpel
Translated from the French by Helen McPhail

"maintains that we (Western civilisation) are about at the end of our technological tether and due for decline . . . entertaining and provocative"
New Scientist

"readable and provocative"
Dr A. G. Keller, Senior Lecturer in History of Science, University of Leicester, England

VISIONS FOR THE 21ST CENTURY
Edited by Sheila Moorcroft

"This book should form the basis of study in any place of learning that prides itself on being concerned for the real education of future generations."
Resurgence

"Worth reading for the essay by Noriko Hama alone."
Professor Charles Handy, Author of *The Age of Un-reason*, *The Empty Raincoat*, *Understanding Organisations*, and *The Future of Work*

About the Author

NORIKO HAMA studied international economics at Hitotsubashi University in Tokyo. Having graduated from the university in 1975, she joined the Mitsubishi Research Institute where she has addressed a variety of macroeconomic issues ranging from the United States economy to financial deregulation in Japan.

In 1990 Ms. Hama was appointed to the post of the Institute's first resident economist and chief representative in London. In this capacity she covers macroeconomic developments in Europe, as well as commenting on events in Japan. Ms. Hama writes regularly on current issues in newspapers and economic journals. She is a frequent commentator for the BBC's World Service Radio and Television broadcasts, as well as other current affairs programmes such as the CNN's World Business News and BBC's *Newsnight*.

Publications include a co-authored book on the evolution of the US dollar's position in the world monetary system since the 1930s, *Can the Dollar Recover?*, Nihon-Hyoronsha (1992, Japan), and a contribution to *Visions for the 21st Century*, Adamantine Press (1992, UK) and Praeger Publishers (1992, USA).

ISBN 0-275-95582-6

9 0000>

9 780275 955823

HARDCOVER BAR CODE